Irish History

*An Enthralling Journey Through Ireland's
Past and Legendary Myths*

Free limited time bonus

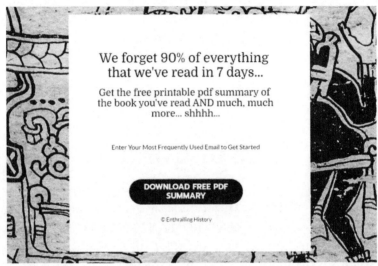

We forget 90% of everything
that we've read in 7 days...

Get the free printable pdf summary of
the book you've read AND much, much
more... shhhh...

Enter Your Most Frequently Used Email to Get Started

**DOWNLOAD FREE PDF
SUMMARY**

© Enthralling History

Stop for a moment. We have a free bonus set up for you. The problem is this: we forget 90% of everything that we read after 7 days. Crazy fact, right? Here's the solution: we've created a printable, 1-page pdf summary for this book that you're reading now. All you have to do to get your free pdf summary is to go to the following website: https://livetolearn.lpages.co/enthrallinghistory/

Or, Scan the QR code!

Once you do, it will be intuitive. Enjoy, and thank you!

Table of Contents

Part 1: History of Ireland

An Enthralling Overview of Major Events and Figures in Irish History

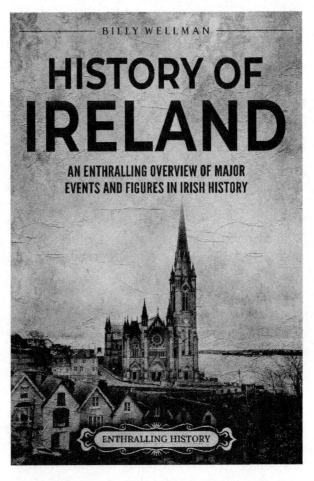

Introduction: Lost Tales from an Irish Past

To say that Irish history is long is perhaps an understatement. The earliest evidence of human habitation is believed to go as far back as 10,500 BCE. It is said that at some distant point in Ireland's prehistory, a group of hunter-gatherers migrated from Scotland and moved into northeastern Ireland during the Stone Age. The archaeological record suggests that the early settlers set up shop in what is now Ireland's Antrim County around the year 6000 BCE.

It is still debated exactly how humans arrived in Ireland. Some scholars have theorized that a land bridge might have existed and that they simply walked across from various parts of Britain. Others insist these settlers sailed across the narrow strait of the North Channel in small makeshift boats.

A few thousand years later, these bold settlers merged with a new wave of Neolithic migrants. This group left huge megalithic monuments similar to England's famous Stonehenge. Many of these monuments can be found scattered about Ireland's County Meath. Just like their more famous contemporary, Stonehenge, these monuments demonstrated a rather advanced understanding of astronomy and how it related to the local environment.

These monuments are located in eastern Ireland's Boyne Valley, a place that is absolutely rich in archaeological evidence. The site has since been dubbed "Newgrange," and the constructed work found there is called the Newgrange monument. It is referred to as such because it was in the vicinity of the "newer" grange (farms) that were utilized by monks from nearby Mellifont Abbey.

The Newgrange monument is thought to have been built by Neolithic farmers around 3200 BCE. The monument stands about 43 feet tall and is around 279 feet in diameter. Interestingly, the interior chambers are constructed in such a way that they are perfectly aligned with the sunrise during the winter solstice. Anyone who happened to walk through the passageway at this time would be greeted by brilliantly illuminating rays of winter sunshine.

Although comparisons have been made to England's Stonehenge, in many ways, this complex is quite similar to the large Native American burial mounds found in North America. It also likely served a similar purpose too, since it is believed this site served as a tomb as well as an astronomical calendar.

These ancient residents of Ireland were quite good at tracking the stars and planets that traversed the skies. Unfortunately, they were not quite so savvy when it came to documenting their own history. As such, much of what has been speculated about them devolves into theories and guesswork. However, the artifacts that they left us clearly indicate they were an intelligent and thoughtful people. They still manage to loom large in tales from a lost Irish past.

Chapter 1: The Celtic Era: Ancient Ireland

"Love is never defeated, and I could add, the history of Ireland proves it."
-Pope John Paul II

If one is to consider Ireland's past, it does not take long before the notion of Celtic culture rises to the forefront of one's mind. Even today, the mystique of Celtic culture in Ireland looms large. There is, of course, Celtic music and dance, which has captivated countless souls, not just in Ireland but also all across the globe. The demand for all things Celtic is indeed high today. But when exactly did the actual Celtic era of ancient Ireland begin?

Although the date is not known for sure, it has been suggested that the period of Celtic Ireland began around 1000 BCE. The Celts first hailed from western Europe and from there pushed onward into Ireland.

It seems that the Celts built much of their civilization and culture on what had already been in place, such as the aforementioned Newgrange monument.

Newgrange.

This is a perfect example of newcomers making use of an older monument for their own purposes. Historians widely agree that the monuments are so ancient (some speculate that they are even older than the pyramids of Egypt) that they could not have been built by the Celts. Even so, after the Celts moved into the region, they made use of it. The Celts left their own unique signature on this ancient megalithic site by way of Celtic spirals, which can be seen all throughout this megalithic compound.

The Celtic spiral is a piece of artwork that represents the Celtic view of life being cyclical. The Celts felt that everything had a cycle, just like the seasons, which go through repetitive cycles of growth, decay, death, and rebirth. They viewed their lives as being caught up in this repetitive cycle of multiple phases of existence.

The Celts also seem to have co-opted Neolithic gods known as the Tuatha as part of their own beliefs and eventually transformed them into their own deities. From the legends of the Tuatha de Danann, the Irish derived tales of enigmatic little people sometimes referred to as the wee folk, the fair folks, or fairies (also spelled as faeries).

Fairies in Irish folklore can range from J. R. R. Tolkien-styled elves who live in wooded sanctuaries to the leprechaun guarding his pot of gold to menacing goblins or, even worse, the fearsome banshee who haunts our worst nightmares with her cries.

The origin of fairies is not exactly known, but Irish folklore seems to suggest they came from over the sea after an earthquake, leading some to ponder if they could have been shipwrecked survivors from the lost island of Atlantis. Even odder, however, are Irish legends stating that the fairies descended onto the island from so-called "cloud ships."

Yes, that is right. There are legends pointing to the origin of fairies as being from somewhere up in the clouds. These creatures eventually descended down to Earth at some distant point in the past like otherworldly enchanted explorers. The celebrated tale of the "Ever-Living Ones" from Irish folklore famously speaks of the fair folk landing their "cloud" on the Emerald Isle. As one can imagine, proponents of ancient astronaut theory have had a field day with these legends over the years.

The Celts not only made use of these ancient sites, but they also coexisted fairly well with those who were already in place. The Celtic people essentially became a very strong minority in the region. Their influence would rise and fall with the new influxes of other people groups in Ireland. However, this all depended on the region and the people groups present there. The Celts likely experienced periods of peace and war. Eventually, the Celts displaced the native inhabitants, assimilating them or driving them off, allowing the Celts to become the most dominant people group on the island.

The Celtic people's governmental system was based on the monarchy. This was a locally based system, meaning there was not a king of the whole of Ireland, at least at first.

The Celts made use of ring forts to fortify the rule of those charged with stewardship. Each ring fort had its own ruler. These many kings would have a profound influence on Ireland.

One of the more interesting things about this complex monarchy of many rulers was that it was not based on hereditary. It was actually based on an election system.

Ireland would come to have about one hundred of these small kingdoms. These small principalities were then grouped into five larger conglomerates, which would become the basic provinces of Ireland: Ulster, Meath, Leinster, Munster, and Connacht.

Eventually, the provinces were governed by a so-called "High King," who would be centered in one province but have overarching authority over the others. This system tended to foster much infighting and discord. One potential claimant to the throne of the high king would fight for his position with others, and the coalitions behind the claimants struggled against each other.

This state of affairs often left Ireland in a state of disunity. Even though the warriors of Ireland were fierce and more than ready to fight off Romans, Vikings, and the English, their own lack of unity left them facing constant domestic turmoil.

Interestingly, by the time of the Romans, even though England was placed under the control of the Roman Empire, Ireland was considered out of bounds and not worth the effort. During the days of the Roman Republic, Julius Caesar landed on the southern coast of Britain on two different occasions, once in 55 BCE and again in 54 BCE. However, he never went near Ireland.

According to Roman historian Tacitus, it was not until the middle of the 1st century CE that Ireland was on the minds of the Roman armies. Roman General Gnaeus Julius Agricola (who just so happened to be Tacitus's father-in-law) ranged through the coasts of southern Scotland. At one point, he could see the shores of Ireland in the distance. Tacitus goes on to relate that Agricola claimed that all he needed was a single Roman legion and the authority to use it to easily seize the new land he saw.

Britain had plenty of resources to keep the Romans occupied, such as its lead and tin deposits. Ireland, on the other hand, simply was not viewed as being worth the effort. Ireland did not have the resources the Romans needed. For the most part, the Irish inhabitants did not bother the Romans, although piracy did occur. Why waste perfectly good Roman men in taking an island that, frankly, was not desired?

The Romans had enough on their hands with Britain. They faced multiple uprisings and rebellions in the region. Despite the Romans' best attempts, they never managed to get all of Britain under their control. The Scottish tribes were a particular thorn in the Roman Empire's side. Roman Emperor Hadrian famously built up a wall to demarcate the claimed Roman domain.

It is not entirely clear whether or not the Irish Celts made a habit of raiding Roman sites after the wall was first put up. Writer and historian Paul F. State has speculated as much due to the fact that Roman artifacts dating back to the 1st century CE have been found in Ireland. State has speculated these items might have been stolen from the Romans after Celts raided Roman bases on the frontiers of Roman Britain. However, these items very well could have been received through trade.

There is evidence that the Irish themselves attempted to insert their own colonies in parts of Britain. During the 4th century CE, Irish settlements were established in Wales. The biggest thrust of this Irish invasion force hailed from Leinster, and it is said that the name of the Llyn Peninsula is derived from this fact.

Claims of Irish inroads into Britain are further backed up by a 10th-century chronicle from an Irish bishop and king from County Tipperary, who once made the following claim:

"The power of the Irish over the Britons was great, and they had divided Britain between them into estates ... And the Irish lived as much east of the sea as they did in Ireland, and their dwellings and royal fortresses were made there ... And they were in that control for a long time even after the coming of St. Patrick to Ireland."

If this account is to be believed, it sounds like powerful Irish rulers were cavorting back and forth over the Irish sea with ease. The way the chronicler puts it, Irish power players were setting up shop in northern Britain with their "dwellings and royal fortresses" and basically lording it over the locals as much as they could.

Celtic pirates were problematic at times for the Romans and native Britons. These pirates targeted coastal towns, villages, and trading ships. They sought riches, livestock, slaves, and valuable commodities, such as precious metals, textiles, and foodstuffs. One of the most famous slaves the Celtic pirates captured was none other than Saint Patrick.

The Celts, in general, were skilled seafarers and warriors. They used fast and maneuverable vessels, which allowed them to swiftly approach their targets, conduct surprise attacks, and evade pursuit. Despite lacking advanced navigation tools, they were still remarkable navigators. They observed the skies, landmarks, currents, and winds to navigate the seas.

In ancient Ireland, Celtic society was organized into a hierarchical structure, with warriors occupying a prominent position. Warriors were highly esteemed for their bravery, skill in combat, and loyalty to their leaders. They underwent rigorous training from a young age, learning combat techniques, weapon proficiency, and tactics. The most popular Celtic weapons were swords, spears, javelins, shields, and bows and arrows. Celtic warriors employed various tactics. They were known for their skill in close combat, and they often relied on hit-and-run tactics or ambushes to get the upper hand.

The Celtic tribes were known for their warrior spirit and fierce independence, which gave the Romans pause when it came to invading Ireland. The Romans nearly launched an invasion of Ireland proper. Plans were made in 81 CE by an ambitious Roman general—the aforementioned Agricola—only for the plans to be canceled by a doubtful Emperor Domitian, who considered the venture too risky and not worth the effort.

Domitian realized he would need quite a bit of manpower for such a feat and prudently understood that Rome's legions were stretched too thin as it was. He recognized that he needed those troops at the ready should other fires erupt on other Roman frontiers.

Even so, the influence of Rome could still be felt in Ireland, even if the island was not being actively occupied by Roman troops. Coins, for example, dating back to the reign of the aforementioned Hadrian (r. 117 CE-138 CE) are still being found scattered along the eastern shores of the Irish coast. Once again, historians debate whether these coins were received through trade or raid, but either way, the influence of the Romans is clear.

The Romans give us our first glimpses into the Irish historical record. The Celts in Ireland had a written language (Ogham), but it is not clear when this language was created. Most scholars believe it was invented in the 4th century CE, while others insist it was created in the 1st century BCE. If the latter is true, the Celts either did not keep written records due to a strong belief in oral traditions or these records were destroyed. Nevertheless, their strong oral tradition allowed their history and legends to be recorded, although this occurred much later. And as we know, things get lost or misconstrued when written down centuries after the fact.

Many of these oral legends speak of powerful Irish kings. One of the most famous of these kings was a figure named Cormac mac Airt (sometimes also spelled as Cormac ua Conn). Although it is debated, some scholars—historian Paul F. State being one of them—believed that he was a real king who lived during the 3rd century.

It is said that Cormac mac Airt held court in the ancient Irish city of Tara and had a large army of Fianna, an elite military guard made up of warriors who hailed from the Irish nobility. If true, this powerful Irish king of legend would have lived during one of the most pivotal times in both Irish and Roman history. He would have reigned over Ireland just as the Romans were bumping shoulders right up against (but not into) his Irish domain.

At any rate, rather than foreign conquering armies, it would be foreign cultural innovations and, more importantly, philosophical outlooks that would penetrate deep into the Irish world. In the 4th century CE, the Roman Empire underwent a massive conversion to Christianity. It would not be long before missionaries from the Roman Catholic Church arrived on Irish shores.

Chapter 2: The Arrival of Christianity

"I am Patrick, a sinner and very ignorant man. I declare that I have been appointed as a bishop in Ireland—and I believe that I have received this position from God himself. I live as a stranger and exile here among barbarians and pagans because of my love for God. He is my witness that this is true. I have never wanted to speak harshly and sternly, but the zeal of God and the truth of Christ have forced me to do it for the sake of my neighbors and children, for whom I gave up my homeland, my family, and my very life until my death. I live for my God to teach unbelievers, if I am worthy, even if some people hate me."

-Saint Patrick

Interestingly, even though it was England who benefited the most from Roman occupation, with the people there enjoying paved roads, efficient methods of government, and Roman laws, Ireland would become the center of the Roman Catholic faith. After the fall of the Roman Empire, Ireland's backwardness and lack of roads actually enabled it to become a kind of refuge for Christianity.

Unlike much of the world at the time, Ireland was hard to reach and, therefore, hard to threaten. Christian missionaries first began to make trips to Ireland in the 3rd century, but it was a 5th-century missionary by the name of Patrick who would make the biggest inroads.

Patrick hailed from a wealthy Roman family. He was the son of a Roman magistrate by the name of Calpurnius. Calpurnius was also apparently a deacon in the local church where Patrick grew up. Patrick was likely poised to follow in his father's footsteps when fate intervened. As a young man, Patrick was kidnapped by a group of Irish pirates.

Kidnapping wealthy young Romans had been a tradition about as old as Rome itself. One of the most famous Roman rulers, Julius Caesar, had even been kidnapped by pirates, although this happened hundreds of years before Saint Patrick's time. Typically, the kidnappers wanted money from the wealthy relatives of those they had taken. Once a ransom was paid, they would release the people they held in captivity.

But in the case of Patrick, his captors were not looking for ransom. Instead, they sold him off to the highest bidder. Patrick was purchased and enslaved. He was made to work as a shepherd for six years before he finally escaped. After he had returned, Patrick shocked his friends and family by deciding to return to Ireland of his own free will as a missionary.

According to some accounts, he supposedly heard a voice telling him, "We beseech you to come and walk amongst us once more." Patrick understood this as a direct command to go back to Ireland to preach the gospel and that was what he did. He arrived back in Ireland in 432 CE and used the rest of his time on Earth preaching to the Irish.

He would spend around thirty years in Ireland, preaching the gospel throughout the Emerald Isle. He not only achieved to attract many converts to the faith, but he also established churches that would remain lasting focal points for the religion, as well as the larger society as a whole. By the time of Saint Patrick's passing, churches could be found all across the Irish landscape.

One of the reasons for Saint Patrick's success was his deep understanding of Ireland, its people, its civic structure, and its culture. Patrick was a keen observer, and during his captivity in Ireland, he had learned much. He put this knowledge of the inner workings of Ireland to good use when he set about establishing a lasting Christian foothold.

For example, Patrick understood the nature of multiple rulers in multiple regions ruled by an overarching high king. He did not seek to disrupt this system. On the contrary, he worked carefully within its framework and made adjustments when necessary so that the churches he established could exist in harmony with local leadership.

Saint Patrick was especially in good with the leaders of Armagh. Armagh is an ancient city in Ireland that dates back to at least the 1st century CE. It was a sacred site for pagan worshipers. In Patrick's day,

Armagh was still viewed as a site of significance, so it only made sense for him to try and make it a focal point for Irish Catholicism.

The fact that Saint Patrick had ingratiated himself with the leaders of Armagh primed this region to become very prominent in the Irish Church; this prominence is still firmly intact to this very day. The city of Armagh itself would become the centerpiece of St. Patrick's mission, with his efforts spreading out in a circle from there.

Following in Saint Patrick's example, many Irish bishops maintained close relationships with the most important ruling families of Ireland. Soon, the church structure of Ireland is said to have basically "mirrored" the civic structure that was already in place.

Saint Patrick and his contemporaries were also keen not to try to excise much of the already existing Irish culture and folklore. As long as the native beliefs could be made somewhat compatible or, at the very least, did not present a significant threat to the Christian religion, Patrick and his immediate contemporaries did not seem to trouble themselves too much with the fact that Irish Christians still believed in fairies and leprechauns.

There is a rather persistent legend that Saint Patrick drove the snakes from Ireland. He supposedly stood on top of a hill and ordered the snakes to leave; true believers still insist that they did. Most scholars believe this is a myth, though. Geologists back up the sheer impossibility of this divine task, not because Saint Patrick was not up for it but because it is not believed Ireland ever had snakes to begin with.

It is believed that after the ice retreated from the last Ice Age, the subsequent Irish Sea that separates Ireland from Britain presented too formidable a barrier for any snakes to cross. Although this theorized reason for Ireland being snake-free is often presented (for lack of a better term) as gospel, we would be wise to remember that it is still just a theory. If people wish to believe that Saint Patrick is the reason Ireland has no snakes, they will likely hold fast to their own theory as well.

Another interesting thing about the Christianization of Ireland is the way that it allowed local traditions to integrate with Christian ideas. For example, missionaries like Patrick pointed to Ireland's celebrated three-leaf clovers (shamrocks) as an example of the Trinity.

According to legend, it is said that Saint Patrick spoke of how the shamrock sprouted three leaves from the same source just like God, who was a triune entity that likewise emerged from the same eternal source.

Saint Patrick was speaking of complex subjects to the Irish, so the utilization of a familiar visual aid in the form of a shamrock likely would have made a lot more sense to them. We do not have firm evidence that this comparison happened, but if Saint Patrick or any other Roman Catholic missionary did such a thing, it really would not be surprising. There are examples of these sorts of attempts to bridge perceived cultural divides all throughout Christian history.

Christianity introduced much that Ireland had been lacking in terms of civilization. Christianity finally introduced a viable writing system to the Irish. It is true that the Celts had their own runic system, but it was not well established, and Celtic runes could hardly compete with the Latin alphabet that the Christians brought with them.

Due to this influx of Christian high learning, as well as the relative seclusion of Ireland, Ireland became an unlikely safeguard of culture and civilization after the fall of the Roman Empire and throughout the so-called Dark Ages.

Saint Patrick was keen to encourage monastic life. Several monasteries and countless monks, who were dedicated to studying the Bible in seclusion, began to pop up all over Ireland. These monasteries were not only centers of learning but also—as we will dive into a bit more in depth shortly—important focal points of civic society. The monasteries created a solid set of rules by which the surrounding communities would come to live.

St. Kevin's Monastery in Wicklow County built in the 500s.
Schcambo at English Wikipedia, CC BY 3.0 <https://creativecommons.org/licenses/by/3.0>, via Wikimedia Commons; https://commons.wikimedia.org/wiki/File:Glendalough_monastery.jpg

These monks were not always shut up in their monasteries either. They periodically went around to preach the gospel and generally did their best to keep the flame of Christianity alive.

The Irish even managed to revitalize Christianity in western Europe when it was in decline. Ireland paid back the missionary favor by sending homegrown saints abroad, such as the bold and eloquent Columba, who left Ireland in the 6th century.

Columba was born in 521 in County Donegal in Ulster. During his time in Ireland, he planted many monasteries and aided his fellow believers in any way he could. He would leave Ireland to preach abroad in 563.

It is easy to assume that his sudden departure was due to his own zeal to spread the gospel, but according to historians, it was actually a bit more complicated than that. There is no doubt that religious zeal to evangelize was a part of it, but there were some other factors at work as well.

Just prior to leaving Ireland, Columba had gotten into a major row with the local powers that be over a prized manuscript (some traditions suggest it was the Vulgate/Latin translation of the scripture) that he had apparently copied without authorization.

The other main job of monks in monasteries was to serve as scribes. Prior to the invention of the printing press, many monks spent much of their entire lives painstakingly copying books and other written texts by hand.

This is apparently what Columba did with the document in question. Another member of the Irish clergy, Saint Finian, was not too happy about it. Upon learning of Columba's unauthorized copying, he ordered him to hand over the document.

Finnian was so irate he took the matter up with the high king of Ireland, Diarmait mac Cerbaill. Both Finnian and Columba ended up taking their case before the king. Finnian argued that it was wrong for Columba to copy the manuscript without his permission, whereas Columba argued that it was wrong for Finnian to try and hold the scripture hostage. Columba basically argued that the document should be accessible to everyone and that he or anyone else should be able to copy it at any time.

Intriguing to think that such arguments were being made before the modern notion of copyright infringement existed. The high king used his own common sense to formulate a ruling on the matter. He supposedly reasoned that just as a calf belongs to a cow, a copy of a book belongs to the original owner of the book. The high king decided that it was indeed Saint Columba who was in the wrong.

This ruling caused much rancor between Columba and High King Diarmait mac Cerbaill. Some historians believe that Columba might have taken his overseas evangelizing mission as a kind of "penance" for the distress that had erupted. If anything, it was likely a good excuse just to get away from all of the drama.

Whatever the case may be, he left with twelve fellow pilgrims. Columba's first stop on this journey was the island of Iona, just west of Scotland. This monastery would go on to become a celebrated site for pilgrims, but upon his arrival, it was ground zero for an ideological battle between Irish Christians and pagans for it was here that he encountered those who were of the Druid faith.

Druidism dates back to some point in antiquity. The first real mention of them was by Julius Caesar, who encountered Celtic Druids during the first ill-fated Roman invasion of Britain. Caesar's most prominent recollection of this mysterious religion was that it engaged in a form of human sacrifice. It has been said that Druids would put people inside giant wicker statues and burn them alive as a sacrifice to their deities.

Columba apparently encountered some of the Druid holdouts and did everything he could to convert those who still practiced Druidism. He also sought to convert local leaders among the Picts, a predominant people group in the region at the time. Columba was successful in this aim, as he managed to persuade King Brude of the Picts into becoming a Christian.

By the time of Columba's death in 597, he had reached much of Scotland, as well as northern England. His influence even managed to extend as far afield as the Orkney Islands.

By this point, the Western Roman Empire had long since fallen, and much of western Europe was in upheaval. The fact that Columba and his followers were able to carry on the message of Roman Catholicism, even once the Western Roman Empire was no more, stands as a great testament of the strength of the Irish brand of Christianity. The calm steady hand of Columba did much to steward a battered and weary flock through these difficult times.

As mentioned, monasteries served as a focal point for societal change in the surrounding cultures. In 697, about one hundred years after Columba's passing, a conference of bishops led by a priest named

Adomnan of Iona hashed out the "Law of Innocents." This law instituted important safeguards for women and children

For example, the law insisted that children should not be turned into child soldiers and forced to fight in wars. The law also stipulated that women should not be assaulted and subjected to violence. We would likely consider such things as a given in modern times, but without the influence of these bishops in making sure these basic human rights were enforced, this might not have been the case back then.

Interestingly, the law also covered Christian priests themselves. Along with women and children, clerics were considered innocent non-combatants who should not be forced into altercations.

Saint Patrick wrote at length about the protection of innocent life back in his day. In one of his letters, which has managed to survive throughout the centuries, he speaks passionately about some of the terrible loss of life he had witnessed. This epistle, which was entitled "Letter to the Soldiers of Coroticus," was aimed at a particular British ruler whose soldiers had severely transgressed against some of his flock.

In the letter, Patrick stated:

"I have composed and written these words with my own hand, to be taken, sent, and delivered to the soldiers of Coroticus. I don't call them my countrymen or blessed Roman citizens, because by their evil deeds they have become fellow citizens with demons. They act in the same way as our enemies and live in death as allies of the Irish and the apostate Picts. They are blood-thirsty men yearning for the blood of innocent Christians, the very ones I brought to life in God and confirmed in Christ. The day after these men cruelly cut down with their swords my newly baptized—they were still clothed in their white garments and had anointing oil on their foreheads—I sent a letter to them by the hand of a holy priest I had trained since his youth, along with some clerics. I asked that they return the baptized captives along with some of the goods they had stolen, but they laughed at them. I don't know who I should weep for more, whether it be the ones killed, those captured, or the men trapped so completely in the devil's snares. For whoever commits sin is the slave of sin and will be known as a child of the devil."

Saint Patrick was disgusted with the wanton violence he saw in Ireland, and he went on to state:

"So let all who fear God know that these men are strangers to me and to Christ my God, the one I serve as an ambassador. They are murderers of fathers and brothers, ravaging wolves who devour the people of God as if they were bread. As scripture says: 'The wicked have destroyed your law, O Lord,' the same law that our merciful and kind God has established in Ireland in these last days."

It is interesting to note the apocalyptic tone that Saint Patrick takes. Christians have been stating that the end is near ever since the very beginning of the faith. Even though no date has ever been officially set, the Bible states that the end could come at any moment and to watch and wait for certain signs.

Saint Patrick also claimed that he had the authority to voice his concerns about violence, saying, "I am not exceeding my authority for I am one of those men God has called and predestined to preach the gospel in the face of terrible persecutions to the very ends of the Earth, even if our enemy shows his jealousy through the tyrant Coroticus, a man with no respect for God or his priests. For God has chosen priests and given them the greatest, most divine, and sublime power, so that whoever they bind on Earth, they will also be bound in heaven."

Patrick is saying that, just like the pope, he holds an important office. And thanks to the efforts of Saint Patrick and others, the church became a predominant focal point of the Irish world at this time.[1] During much of the 7th and 8th centuries, the church would be the center of rule-making, education, and the economy.

The great castle-like monasteries stored up tremendous amounts of treasure. As writer and historian Peter Neville put it, "The great monasteries of the day, rather than the kings and princelings who fought for domination throughout the pre-Viking period, were the main economic units in this society. A great monastery like Durrow could have many thousands of tenants, dependent churches with their estates, and vast wealth."[2]

Because of this, the bishop was considered a ruler of sorts, ruling over his own monastic kingdom. The secular leaders of Ireland tended to work hand in hand with the clergy. They expected the clergy to essentially serve as representatives of the communities where they served.

---

[1] An interesting side note here is that Patrick has never been formally canonized by a pope. Nevertheless, many Christians refer to Patrick as Saint Patrick.

[2] Neville, Peter. *A Traveller's History of Ireland.* 1992.

The notion that bishops would serve a dual purpose as community leaders was realized by none other than Saint Patrick and was duly noted in the so-called "Riaghail Phatraic" ("Law of Patrick").

Scholar Peter Neville went into some detail about this in his book *A Traveller's History of Ireland*. As Peter Neville noted, this particular bit of monastic legislation decreed, "There shall be a chief bishop of each tuath to ordain their clergy, to consecrate their churches, to be confessor to rulers and superiors, and to sanctify and bless their children after baptism."

It really should not be surprising that such a hierarchy might have been established. The pope, after the fall of the Western Roman Empire, was basically considered the ruler of his own realm. Even today, the pope is considered the head of his own miniature realm within Rome, now known as Vatican City.

The "Law of Patrick" acknowledged such an arrangement and sought to reproduce it on a smaller scale in Ireland, with the bishops ruling their own small monastic domains. Since the bishops were considered rulers in their own right, the monastery was a kind of nerve center for the community. They were intermediaries between the commoners and the rulers of Ireland. With no army of their own, these monastic domains were the soft underbelly of Irish administration. It probably should not surprise us that invaders such as the Vikings would choose to attack them.

Ruthless bands of Vikings would swoop down on Ireland, entirely disregarding the "Law of Innocents" as they killed many they encountered, robbed monasteries of their treasure, and did their best to strike fear in the hearts of those they encountered. The Vikings were a scary bunch, and their arrival would alter the course of Irish Christianity in many profound and unpredictable ways.

With the arrival of the Vikings, Ireland's relative peace and prosperity would come to an abrupt end when the Irish were hit with an entirely unexpected onslaught from the north. Their antagonists could care less about Christianity. In their opinion, it would have been just fine if the religion were snuffed out entirely (although their feelings about the religion would change as time passed).

Chapter 3: Viking Invasions in Early Medieval Ireland

"The Irish do not want anyone to wish them well—they want everyone to wish their enemies ill."

-Harold Nicolson

As much as Ireland might have been a refuge for Christianity and learning during the Dark Ages, that relative sense of security would come to a shocking end when Vikings from the cold north launched an unexpected and devastating attack on a Christian monastery in Lindisfarne. The attack occurred in 793 CE on the actual island of Lindisfarne, which is situated just off the coastlines of Northumberland.

While the island is not part of Ireland, it has a long Irish tradition. In 635 CE, St. Aidan, an Irish monk, founded Lindisfarne Monastery. The monastery became a center of great learning. Around 700 CE, a beautiful illuminated Latin manuscript known as the Lindisfarne Gospels was written.

At the time, the attack seemed entirely random. The monks had certainly done nothing to offend these strangers. So, why did it occur? Well, the targeting of Lindisfarne might not have been as random as was once thought. Lindisfarne was a major center of Christian outreach in the region. One of the groups being actively targeted by this outreach was, no doubt, some of the Vikings, who resided farther north in the lands of Scandinavia.

Some scholars believe the Vikings were in the midst of a kind of holy war with the Catholic Church. Prior to this attack on Lindisfarne, Charlemagne the Great, King of the Franks and Lombards, sent an expedition into what is now Denmark and butchered the Norse pagans he found there. He also ordered his troops to burn down one of their sacred trees.

This incident occurred in 772 when Charlemagne's forces were pushing deeper and deeper into what was then known as Saxony. This sacred tree (or pillar) was known as an Irminsul.

It is worth noting that Norse mythology, as well as the Druid mythology of Ireland, places a special emphasis on sacred trees. If it is ever cut down, the Vikings believe Ragnarök (the Norse version of Armageddon) would occur. In Norse mythology, Yggdrasil is a great tree that symbolically represents the universe itself. The Latin variation of Irminsul, in fact, is *universalis columna*, which basically means "column that carries the universe."

When Irminsul, a representation of Yggdrasil, was destroyed, many Vikings took this as a sign that the end times had begun. And it was shortly after all of this that Lindisfarne was burned to the ground.

Could it be a coincidence? There is still a lot of debate on this, but it is plausible that, that from the Viking perspective, pillaging and burning Lindisfarne was just as much one of vengeance as it was for mere plunder.

However, it is incredibly likely that the Vikings chose Lindisfarne because it was isolated and presented an easy target to raid. The attack sent shockwaves through the Christian community. How could anyone kill monks and pillage relics and treasures from a religious center? As has been mentioned, the Vikings followed a different religion, so they obviously did not hold Christianity in as high of a regard. To them, treasure was treasure.

Regardless of why the attack on Lindisfarne happened, Viking attacks increased over the years. Ireland was not spared.

Ireland had long been domestically divided by a system of many kings who were ruled by one high king. The country had its weaknesses, especially disunity. One of the early efforts to thwart these devastating Viking raids was to build a series of watch towers in and around monasteries and other vulnerable installations.

These watch towers provided an eagle-eye view of any approach so that the alarm could be raised. The towers were formidable fortresses and could also serve as places of refuge if need be.

The Vikings, however, were playing for keeps. They soon moved from random raids to launching all-out invasions. The first wave of these occurred in 795. Fast forward to around 836, and the Vikings were launching major inland expeditions.

The Vikings continued to force their way into Ireland until they began to seize tracts of land and settle in the region. It was thanks to the Vikings that the fortified cities of Dublin, Wexford, Waterford, Cork, and Limerick were developed. The Vikings, as fierce as their penchant for fighting was, proved to be great administrators. They quickly turned their settlements into major hubs of commercial trade.

This was most especially the case in Dublin. According to historian Peter F. State, the oldest records of a Viking settlement in the region first emerged in 843 CE. Crude but sturdy structures were erected on the banks of the Liffey River. These likely began as a staging area for Vikings arriving from the north. The Vikings sailed down into the Irish Sea and then into what is now called Dublin Bay, which is the mouth of the Liffey River.

This settlement was soon fortified with earthen barriers and even stone walls. These fortifications allowed Viking ships to come and go with ease, and both raiding and trading was pushed farther inland into the rest of Ireland.

The Vikings thrived and continued to take advantage of the disorganized state of the native Irish. Yet, paradoxically enough, it has been said that it was the very disorganized and decentralized nature of the Irish state that might have spared it from a complete Viking takeover. If there had been just one centralized ruler of Ireland, it would have been pretty easy for a huge Viking army to descend, knock out the power base, and then take over. Without a single centralized ruler, the Vikings had several fires they had to put out at the same time.

Even so, the Irish would soon rally behind one of their own who promised to get rid of the Vikings once and for all. Around the year 1000, a powerful Irish leader by the name of Brian Boru arrived on the scene.

Brian Boru was a skilled leader and warrior who managed to battle his way to the top of Ireland's power structure. Brian was practically born into a state of warfare with his father, Cennetig's, family—the Dal Cais dynasty— duking it out with the Eoganacht dynasty of Munster. Cennetig was successful in this aim, and by the time he perished in 951, his sons,

Mathgamain and Brian Boru, were able to continue the push deeper into Munster.

Mathgamain was double-crossed by his defeated foes, and he died in 976. This left Brian in charge of his family's conquest of Ireland. He did not disappoint, as he soon had control of all of Munster, located in southern Ireland. He then turned his attention to the north, to Ulster. Here, he put down several smaller kings before his attention was turned to Leinster and the Viking stronghold of Dublin.

In 999, Brian Boru managed to put down his most powerful rivals in Leinster and Dublin. By the year 1011, Brian Boru's dominance over Ireland was all but secured. However, it would soon become clear that there was still some unsettled business to take care of. The king of Leinster, Máel Mórda mac Murchada, had already given his submission but simmered with resentment. Once Brian Boru's back was turned, Mael Morda entered into a plot with the Vikings to align his forces with the Viking warlord Jarl Sigurd of Orkney.

In 1014, the Battle of Clontarf was waged just outside of Dublin on Good Friday. A coalition of Irish warriors assembled by Brian Boru smashed into this new threat. Brian Boru was killed in the battle, but his nemesis and rival, Máel Mórda mac Murchada, was also killed. The Vikings in Ireland had been dealt a decisive blow.

However, even though the Vikings were defeated at Clontarf, they remained very much in place. From that moment forward, they would continue the long, drawn-out process of intermingling with the locals. There would be intermarriage and the merging of customs. As historian Paul F. State contends, this new unique phase of Irish culture could be referred to as being "Hiberno-Norse." This blend of cultures and traditions would ultimately stand up to the onslaught of an impending invasion from Normandy, France.

Chapter 4: The Norman Conquest and the Start of Anglo Control

"You that would judge me, do not judge alone this book or that, come to this hallowed place where my friends' portraits hang and look thereon. Ireland's history in their lineaments trace; think where my glory most begins and ends and say my glory was I had such friends."

-William Butler Yeats

The Norman invasion is usually viewed as an invasion of Britain. However, Ireland also faced an invasion, which occurred in May 1169. The Normans, as it turns out, had the same problem that the Vikings had before them.

The Normans very much would have liked to have achieved a knockout blow as they had in England by defeating the high king of Ireland in battle. However, Ireland was once again in a state of disunity during this time, so there was no sole authority figure for the Normans to topple. Even so, the Norman war machine continued to move forward with plans for the seizure of Ireland.

In consideration of all of this, it must be asked what was in it for the Normans. Why did they go to all of the trouble to invade Ireland in the first place?

It seems that one of the primary motivations was that Ireland, despite its general disunity, boasted a robust trade network, which dated all the way back to the times of the Vikings. This makes sense; after all, the Vikings had turned Dublin into a major trading hub. Dublin was the center of a network that had arms spiraling out as far as Bristol.

Prior to the Norman invasion of Ireland, the Norman invasion of England was led by one of history's most renowned and iconic figures: William the Conqueror. Prior to conquering England, he held the title of the duke of Normandy.

The drama began when the English king, Edward the Confessor, abruptly perished in 1066 without a clear heir to the throne. William was ready to stake a claim since Richard II of Normandy, the deceased King Edward's uncle, was his grandfather.

However, this claim was not recognized in England, and a noble named Harold Godwinson was made king instead. After the English refused to recognize William's claim, he decided to take over by force. This led to a Norman landing and the subsequent Battle of Hastings on October 14th, 1066. This fateful battle would leave Harold dead on the battlefield and his troops defeated. William still had some more fighting to do, but before the year was out, he would be hailed as king. He was officially crowned on Christmas Day (December 25th), 1066.

William the Conqueror would perish in 1087, but his Norman successors led the charge into Ireland. Between the years 1169 and 1171, the Normans managed to score several wins against the Irish.

During this period, all of southeastern Ireland was besieged, and Wexford was taken by the Normans. The Normans and their English auxiliaries were aided in their conquest by superior equipment. The Norman armies were outfitted with the latest weapons and armor, whereas the Irish armaments were typically second-rate.

The Norman and English troops, for example, had formidable crossbows, which they used to decimate Irish infantry. The Irish, on the other hand, were still using primitive slings to hurl rocks at their opponents. As writer and historian Peter Neville put it, "The Normans had heavily-mailed knights who fought on horseback and were supported by well-trained Welsh crossbowmen, whereas the native Irish still used slings and stones for weaponry, and when they did ride horses, rode them bareback."[3]

The outmatched Irish defenders were easily defeated. The Normans had a series of easy victories in the southeastern reaches of Ireland between the years 1169 and 1171. Of particular significance was the

---

[3] Neville, Peter. *A Traveller's History of Ireland.* 1992.

Normans' taking of Dublin in 1170.

At this time, England was ruled by King Henry II, who was a modernizer and sought to pull Britain out of the Dark Ages. King Henry II was also a vigorous champion of expansion. But he had some ulterior motives in doing so.

In 1171, Henry became embroiled in religious controversy after his leading antagonist in regard to the faith—Thomas Becket—was killed. King Henry II and Thomas Becket had once been close friends. The king even appointed Becket as an archbishop. Things did not go quite as planned, however. Becket managed to stoke the king's wrath by vigorously arguing over what the exact relationship should be between the church and state.

The king's relationship with Becket continued to deteriorate. This discord came to a terrifying and violent head in December 1170 when knights loyal to the king burst into Canterbury Cathedral and forcibly laid their hands upon Becket. It has been said that they initially intended to arrest him, but during the course of the struggle, one of the knights sliced off a good portion of the top of Becket's head with their sword. Becket was left to bleed to death in the church. This bloody act generated quite a bit of scandal.

Henry was suspected of having been behind the hit, and he was actually condemned by the church for carrying out the murder. He was told to embark upon a "suitable deed" to vindicate himself, and it seems that the conquest of Ireland was the quest that he settled upon.

However, once Ireland was militarily subdued, Henry proved to be too distracted to adequately administer it. He tried to leave this task to subordinates and ultimately placed his own son, John, in charge in 1177. The only trouble was that his son was only nine at the time! This meant that the true power would lay with those who advised John, and these men often had competing loyalties and motivations.

Nevertheless, in 1185, King Henry went as far as to petition the pope to have John recognized as the king of Ireland. John paid a visit to Ireland in 1185 for the first time and stayed there for several months, observing the antagonism on display between the Norman occupiers and the local Irish leaders. John did not seem to help matters, as his arrogant manners were put on full display before the Irish chieftains. Although this incident is disputed by historians, some accounts claim that he actually pulled on the beards of some of the Irish leaders who came to meet with him. If that story is true, such actions are not endearing, to say the least.

John was more than content to leave the actual rule of Ireland up to others. After King Henry II passed in 1189, the English crown went to John's older brother, Richard the Lionheart. Lionheart was the famed Crusader who led an army to the Middle East and fought Sultan Saladin of Egypt and Syria to a standstill.

Richard would perish in 1199, making his brother John the new king of England, as well as the supposed king of Ireland. It was not until 1210 that good old King John, now all grown up, decided to throw his weight around and enforce his rule over Ireland. This enforced rule meant the establishment of a feudal state within Ireland.

Norman occupation saw Irish land, which had been the domain of the Irish chiefs, be divvied up and handed out to English nobility. This actually created a slight problem for King John down the road when some Anglo-Norman barons began to grow a bit too big for their britches. In 1210, King John made his way to Dublin to put down any potential opposition and make it clear who was calling the shots. Soon, active fighting erupted with these barons, and John's troops besieged the strategic site of Carrickfergus Castle.

This event led the powerful Anglo-Norman baron named Hugh de Lacy to leave Ireland and head to Scotland. Hugh de Lacy had previously been an important figure and was a main participant in the early stages of the Norman invasion of Ireland under John's father, King Henry II. Hugh de Lacy was also an integral part of pacifying the local Irish, a task that was deemed to have been completed by the year 1175. For his efforts, he had been awarded control of most of County Meath. His abrupt departure for Scotland, however, left his Irish land up for grabs.

King John had his own problems in England in the meantime. Due to the discontent of his own nobles at home, he was forced to sign off on the groundbreaking legal document known as the Magna Carta in 1215. This document ensured that the land-owning subjects of the Crown would be granted a fair hearing in court if a dispute erupted. The Magna Carta also ensured that there would be no unwarranted coercion made against them.

The notion that one should be allowed their day in court and should not be attacked for no reason likely seems like common sense to most of us today. However, these were major milestones in Britain at the time. Prior to signing the Magna Carta, kings could basically do whatever they wanted; now, there were at least some safeguards for the nobility (the rest would have to wait).

After this had been achieved, a balance between the Anglo-Norman rulers of Ireland and the king of England was established. The terms of the Magna Carta were meant to apply to Ireland just as much as England, and a later, more specific charter would be issued in 1217 that noticeably substituted "London" for "Dublin." Otherwise, the charter was much the same.

Not long after King John signed the original Magna Carta, he died. He passed away in 1216 and was succeeded by his young son, Henry III.

Both Henry III and his successor, Edward I, were content to rule Ireland from afar through royal officials. They would not pay an official visit to the region during their respective reigns. King Edward, for his part, did make an effort to at least get the Irish on board with English common law.

Edward sent word in 1277 for his plans to incorporate the Irish into the English civil system, but the Irish were content to stick with their own old legal codes and traditions, so they largely ignored him. This was a setback for effective streamlining governance in Ireland. It left Ireland locked out of the integrated circuitry that ran through early English bureaucracy, which was essentially a forerunner to what would become Parliament.

Locked out of the bureaucratic world, Ireland would have to be ruled by the decree of the king of England. Meanwhile, the Irish had kept up their tradition of a high king, even if the position was a rather toothless one. Brian O'Neill of the powerful O'Neill clan became high king in 1258. But if it is any demonstration of how arbitrary the distinction had become, the title was actually offered to Norway's king in 1263 in an abortive attempt to gain Norse support against the English.

Brian O'Neill was defeated by Anglo-Norman colonists and killed in battle in 1260. Traditionally, this would have been the cue for the Irish to begin the long, troubling process of squabbling amongst themselves for a successor. But rather than looking inward, they ultimately looked outward. In 1263, they offered the high kingship of Ireland to King Haakon IV of Norway.

The fact that the Irish would rather be ruled by a complete outsider in the form of a Norwegian king demonstrates the complete contempt they had for the hated Anglo-Norman landlords and the English king who backed them.

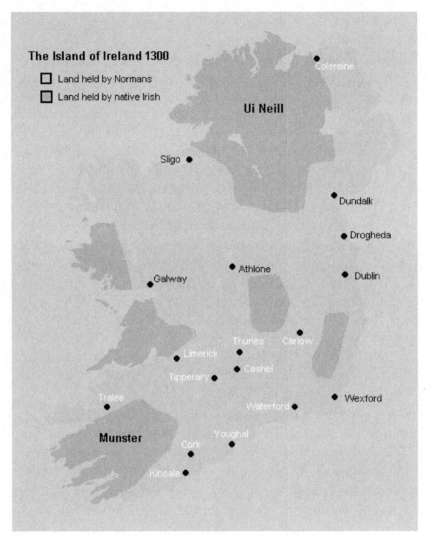

Ireland in 1300.

Ireland's prosperity would rise and fall during this period. Ireland became a big agricultural producer and also specialized in the export of wool. Irish commodities like these were exported to England and many other localities far and wide. The Anglo-Norman landlords profited from these enterprises, leading to the rise of sturdy stone castles, which dotted the landscape.

However, the Irish grew restless. By the end of King Edward I's reign in 1307, the Irish had begun to protest against English (Anglo-Norman) authority. Edward II, who ruled until 1327, dealt with an increasingly agitated Irish public.

Why were the Irish so upset? Well, by this point in Irish history, about half of all of the Anglo-Norman barons were absentee landlords, meaning that they spent more of their time in England, Normandy, or somewhere else rather than in Ireland. You can imagine the frustration of the native Irish. They were being lorded over by people they viewed as foreign usurpers, and these usurpers did not even remain in the country. The Irish landed nobility perhaps hated this situation the most since they were the ones who suffered the ramifications of what this absenteeism did to the land. The Irish who managed to hang on to their lands faced the specter of very bad neighbors in the form of these lax Anglo-Norman landlords.

The English also began to enforce restrictions against Anglo-Normans who decided to remain in Ireland and went "native," meaning they adopted Irish customs, married into Irish families, and essentially became Irish themselves in the process. England did not want this. Its goal was to Anglicize Ireland and diminish Irish culture. These acts essentially amounted to cultural genocide (the eradication of a whole culture), and their actions might be a bit hard for us to fathom today. Concerns over this fraternization and the feared influence of Irish culture on the English led to the infamous Statutes of Kilkenny in 1366.

The statutes were actually instituted by King Edward III's son, Lionel. The prince marched into Ireland with an army, but he did not have too much luck with martial might at the time. Instead, he decided to achieve what he failed to do in blatant conquest with bureaucratic legislation.

He convened a conference in the town of Kilkenny and laid out statutes to enforce English customs on the Anglo-Irish. Today, we would likely consider these statutes to be blatantly discriminatory against the Irish. The statutes stated that the English were not only to refrain from marrying the Irish but were also to basically minimize all relations with the locals.

It was forbidden to speak the Irish language, and people were not allowed to follow any local rules or customs. Prior to this, the close proximity of Anglo-Irish among the native Irish had created a sense of familiarity; these statutes sought to seed alienation and fan the flames of animosity between them.

Considering previous efforts to better streamline Ireland into Britain, these statutes seem horribly counterproductive. Lionel's statutes were mostly ignored, just as much as his army had been. It was not until a decade later that King Richard II was able to raise a formidable enough body of troops to actually make the statutes the law of the land.

Richard II was deposed in 1399, but the statutes continued to have an effect. By 1450, the only real portion of Ireland that the king of England had real control over was the so-called "English Pale," which consisted of Dublin and some twenty miles of surrounding land. English control over the rest of Ireland remained aspirational at best.

Chapter 5: Tudors and Plantations

"I find that I sent wolves not shepherds to govern Ireland, for they have left me nothing but ashes and carcasses to reign over!"

-Queen Elizabeth I

Of all of the outside forces that threatened to dominate Ireland, the most formidable would prove to be England's Tudor dynasty. The Tudor dynasty, kicked off by Henry VII in 1485, would begin a renewed interest on the part of the English in bringing Ireland to heel. In total, the Tudors would wage a succession of four all-out wars to bring Ireland fully into its sphere of influence. But before we get into all of that, it would be a good idea to understand a bit of the background of the Tudor dynasty itself.

It all began back in 1483 when England's King Edward IV perished. Richard of Gloucester momentarily seized power after deposing Edward's twelve-year-old son, who was also named Edward. Richard was successfully challenged in 1485 by a rich nobleman named Henry Tudor. Henry was able to raise an army and put an end to Richard's reign, securing the throne for himself. Henry Tudor then became known as Henry VII.

King Henry VII did not have much of an impact on Ireland, but his successor, King Henry VIII, most certainly would. King Henry VIII tried to fully enforce and greatly expand upon the aforementioned Statutes of Kilkenny.

So, who exactly was this overbearing Henry VIII? In order to understand his policies, we must understand the man. Henry VIII was coronated on June 24th, 1509. His forebearer, although an able steward in many ways as it pertained to domestic policies, was not the most charming and rarely engaged the public. However, his flamboyant successor, Henry VIII, was different. He was determined to make a big show of things from the very start.

On his very coronation day, he made sure to create an extravagant display that would capture the public's imagination. He also punished his father's harshest taskmasters—Richard Empson and Edmund Dudley—to the utter delight of British subjects everywhere.

However, all was not well in the household of Henry VIII due to the fact that his wife Catherine seemed entirely unable to produce a son. Having a male heir was considered vital to the British throne in those days, so this was no small matter. Henry VIII agonized over this problem until he finally decided that he would have to put his wife away and find a new one who was capable of producing baby boys.

But how to dismiss Catherine and stay within the bounds of Catholic teaching? That was Henry's number one objective.

He thought about it for some time and seemed to find a unique solution. His eyes sighted the Bible verse Leviticus 20:21, which states, "If a man shall take his brother's wife, it is an impunity: he hath uncovered his brother's nakedness: they shall be childless." For Henry VIII, this verse seemed to give him a reason to put away his wife and an explanation for the state that they were in.

Catherine had been married to Henry's older brother, Arthur, but he perished shortly after they wed. Henry then took it upon himself to marry the widowed Catherine. However, Henry began to think the marriage was cursed because Catherine was unable to give him a son. Catherine did give birth to a daughter, Mary, but having a woman take the throne of England was unheard of at that time.

Henry believed he was within the bounds of scripture to set Catherine aside and that it was the only right thing to do. Indicating that his marriage was a mistake, he sought an annulment to correct the perceived error. He petitioned Pope Clement VIII to oblige him, but the pope was not willing.

This makes sense, though. The pope was torn between his desire to please the king of England, who had been a loyal ally, and Holy Roman Emperor Charles V, who also just so happened to be Catherine of Aragon's nephew. The pope did not wish to alienate either one, so he mostly put off making a decision. Henry ultimately lost his patience with the Catholic Church and sought a unilateral annulment before breaking with the church completely.

Henry issued the Act of Supremacy in 1534, which made him the head of the Church of England. The English monarch would now reign over the state and also the state's religion.

Henry would go on to marry Anne Boleyn, but after she was unable to produce a son, he had her executed in 1536. He then married Jane Seymour. She would produce a male heir, the future King Edward VI, but she perished in 1537, leading Henry to marry Anne of Cleves.

Henry was an obstinate character as it pertained to wives at this point in his life. Upon the first sign of frustration, he had his latest marriage with Anne of Cleves annulled (at least she was able to live in comfort and not face the executioner!). Henry wed Catherine Howard, who lost her head in 1542. That marriage was followed by his marriage to Catherine Parr, his last and final wife, who would remain with Henry until he perished in 1547.

Now that we have covered the infamous backstory of Henry VIII and his many unfortunate wives, we can rewind the narrative a bit to see how this notorious king related to Irish history. The stakes in Ireland were significantly raised just a few years after Henry came to the throne. In 1513, a momentous seat change occurred when Gearóid Óg, also known as Gerald FitzGerald, became the ninth earl of Kildare.

Many are likely not familiar with Gearóid Óg or Kildare, but he and the region he ruled are immensely important. Kildare was a region that bordered the ever-shrinking Anglo-Irish enclave in Dublin known as the Pale. Considered a strategic frontier, it was ruled by warlord-like earls who served as de facto kings of Ireland. King Henry did not like how Gearóid was getting on, and in 1519, Henry ordered him to report to London.

After Gearóid Óg reported to the English monarch, King Henry was not too terribly impressed. By the following year, in May of 1520, he managed to get Gearóid Óg dismissed in favor of Thomas Howard as Lord Deputy. Howard, who was the uncle of both Anne Boleyn and Catherine Howard, immediately began to try his hand at crushing the martial might of rebels in Leinster, Ulster, and the Midlands.

He stood against the powerful O'Neill family. Thomas Howard did not last long and was soon recalled to take part in conflicts against the French. Between 1522 and 1529, there were several dismissals and recalls, with no appointed deputy lasting longer than a couple of years.

After Henry broke with the Catholic Church, all hell broke loose. When Henry issued the Act of Supremacy in 1534, the earl of Kildare, Thomas FitzGerald, known as "Silken Thomas" because of his penchant for fine silk, stood up against Henry, roundly denouncing him as a heretic. The Irish were staunch Catholics, and as such, Silken Thomas was seen as a populist Catholic leader of sorts by the Irish people. Not only that, but he also positioned himself as a potential tool for both the pope and the Holy Roman emperor.

To have such a terrible thorn emerge in his side was an intolerable nuisance for King Henry VIII, and he immediately took action. King Henry VIII sent some 2,300 troops to Ireland, led by Sir William Skeffington. Henry tasked the men with pacifying Kildare.

This group of troops besieged the formidable Maynooth Castle in March 1535. The castle fell, and on March 25th, the English troops wreaked their vengeance on twenty-five prisoners of war who had their heads chopped off outside the toppled fortress walls. Thomas FitzGerald was executed, along with many of his relatives. This was the end of Kildare's power, and the earldom was officially dismantled in 1537.

Since the de facto rule of Kildare was no more, this meant that King Henry VIII would have to take a more direct role in Ireland from here on out. So, he installed a thoroughly English governor, who was backed up by a formidable English garrison of troops. Henry's dominance was made official in 1541 when he was proclaimed "Lord of Ireland."

The previous Irish power players were forced to show their allegiance to Henry. Those who were loyal to the English Crown were made liege lords and given the distinction of being made earls of their domain. Of course, not everyone readily agreed to this. Some decided to defy the ambitions of the English king. These dissenters—at least in King Henry's eyes—were nothing more than rogues and rebels.

One of the most prominent among them was an Irish chieftain named Dubhdara O'Malley. O'Malley had a great fleet of ships, which he made good use of by speedily sailing from one place to another. O'Malley's fleet was even known to sail as far as sympathetic Catholic Spain. To the Irish, O'Malley was a freedom fighter, but to the English, he was a pirate.

However, it was his daughter Grace who would go down in infamy for her stunning raids on English property. They were so stunning that she would be forever be dubbed "Grace O'Malley, the Pirate Queen." Grace began her career early, allegedly sneaking onto one of her dad's ships and pretending to be a cabin boy. Grace grew up, got married to a prominent Irishman named Donal O'Flaherty, and raised a family before she rose to prominence and became a great thorn in England's side.

She and her crew mostly raided merchant ships. Upon boarding the craft, Grace and her followers often demanded the percentage of the value of the goods that the merchant craft carried. If the besieged merchants could not pay up, these pirates simply seized the goods themselves. It may sound terrible that the Irish would ever resort to piracy, but we cannot forget that piracy had been a long-established practice in Ireland. Additionally, King Henry VIII first decided to pick sides, so it is not all that surprising that some of the Irish would "go rogue" and utilize underhanded tactics, such as piracy, in a bid to strike back.

King Henry VIII would perish in 1547 after much of this damage to Ireland had already been done. And what damage are we speaking of? Well, besides usurping ancestral titles from the local Irish, Henry essentially sowed enmity between the local families who bowed to the Crown and those who refused. He also instituted many of the conditions that would lead to unrest and even outright famine in the future.

Henry's immediate successors would begin the colonization process of Ireland through a series of plantations. Henry was initially succeeded by his son, Edward VI. He would only live to be fifteen, and the biggest impact he made during his short tenure was his implementation of the *Book of Common Prayer* to Ireland. It was the first printed book in Ireland that was in English. This was done, of course, under the heavy influence of Edward's Protestant handlers, who wished to convert Irish Catholics to their way of thinking.

Proving how easily the winds of fate could shift, the Protestant-friendly boy king would perish (as would all of Henry's dreams of a long-lived male heir), and Henry's daughter Mary—a diehard Catholic—became queen. She was known as "Bloody Mary" because of her vengeful nature and her bloody reversal of many Protestant policies, which led to hundreds being executed on religious grounds. But despite her penchant for Catholicism, Mary had no patience for a rebellious Ireland. She sought to pacify the Irish by installing plantations in the counties of Laois and Offaly in Ireland in the 1550s. These plantations were supposed to set an "English example," which favored pastoral farming above anything else.

However, the harsh Queen Mary's reign was just about as brief as her ill-fated predecessor. Mary passed away in 1558, opening the door for

Queen Elizabeth to take the throne.

Queen Elizabeth continued the trend of Ireland's colonization by way of plantations. Queen Elizabeth also returned to the Protestant-friendly policies of Edward, which was a great boon to the Protestant minority in Ireland at the time.

But Queen Elizabeth would face a long spate of unrest, which had its roots in the 1559 election of Shane O'Neill as the earl of Tyrone. Shane was the son of the former earl, Conn Bacagh O'Neill. According to Gaelic custom, Shane was the rightful heir. However, the English government in Ireland, headed by Thomas Radclyffe, Earl of Sussex, did not recognize this claim and instead favored his cousin, Brian. The Irish recognized Shane, and he soon brought all of his rivals under his control. He did so by diplomacy when he could, but he did use force when necessary.

Thomas Radclyffe's government in Sussex did not take too kindly to all of this and viewed Shane as an ominous threat to English interests in the region. Fighting ensued, and in 1562, Shane O'Neill was forced to come to London to give an account of his actions. It is said that he begged the queen for mercy and swore that he would, from that point forward, be her loyal servant.

It seems Queen Elizabeth did indeed offer her mercy, as she agreed to recognize Shane as the Earl of Tyrone. By 1564, however, these plans had once again broken down, and Shane again began to launch rebellions against the English. He invaded the Pale and razed Armagh to the ground in 1566. He also drove into Ulster, where he viciously assaulted the Scottish MacDonnells, who had their stronghold there. During this period, Ulster was a hotbed of plantation activity.

Shane was brought to heel in 1567 when he was trounced by the forces of Hugh O'Donnell. But although his rebellion was shattered, O'Neill himself managed to escape.

After he tried to negotiate with the Scots, he met his end. The Scots were actively collaborating with the English at the time and decided it would better serve their interests to have Shane killed. He was summarily executed, and his decapitated head was promptly shipped off to the queen's Lord Deputy, Sir Henry Sidney. Upon receipt of the head, the queen knew that the threat of Shane O'Neill, the former earl of Tyrone, was finally at an end.

However, soon after this revolt against English encroachment was snuffed out, another conflagration erupted in the form of the so-called

"Geraldine Revolt." The revolt is also known as the Desmond Rebellions. This tumult is centered around the FitzGerald family (also referred to as the Geraldines), who controlled Desmond, and their struggle with England. This revolt broke out in 1569 and would last all the way until 1583.

This revolt had two driving forces. First of all, it was sparked by mere jealousy between the Geraldines and the highly influential earl of Ormond, Thomas Butler. It was also due to the hostility that had arisen in regard to the relations of now mostly Protestant England and strongly Catholic Spain.

King Philip II was the king of Spain at the time and had long desired to bring England back to the Catholic fold. Queen Elizabeth had become something of a Protestant champion. England would defend—or at least lend support—to Protestant territories that Spain was at war with, such as the Netherlands. The Irish Catholics wished to link up with Spain as a means to offset their English opponents.

These two driving forces would lead to even more forceful resistance to the English plantation scheme in Ireland. Leading the revolt was James FitzMaurice FitzGerald, who was the cousin of the fifteenth earl of Desmond. FitzMaurice sought to gain international support for a stand against the English.

He was not quite successful, as he did not gain military support from the French or Spanish, but he did manage to gain support from Pope Pius V, who went as far as to have Queen Elizabeth excommunicated. Since Henry VIII had severed England from the dictates of Rome, such things had very little meaning. For the Protestants of England—many of whom viewed the pope as an insufferable tyrant—excommunication could be worn as a badge of honor rather than a sign of disgrace.

In July 1579, FitzMaurice took an army and sent it to smash into the English forces. However, FitzMaurice, for all of his bravery and determination, would perish before he reached his destination.

Was he killed by forces loyal to Queen Elizabeth? Not exactly. FitzMaurice was killed in what seems to be an entirely unrelated scuffle with one of his cousins, Theobald Burke, and his minions.

Although this ambush was unexpected, the accounts of FitzMaurice's last stand are rather riveting. It has been said that he was shot in the chest, and the wound proved to be fatal. But just prior to succumbing to his injuries, the infuriated FitzMaurice used his sword to hack through

Theobald's men until he reached his cousin Theobald himself.

In his fury, FitzMaurice managed to kill Theobald on the spot, running him through with his sword. This would be the last act of the mighty FitzMaurice, as he collapsed and died of his injuries shortly afterward. FitzMaurice stands out as one of the greats of Irish resistance to outside oppression, yet ironically enough, he perished as a victim of Irish infighting.

At any rate, the revolt would peter out a few years later, coming to a close in 1583.

One fearsome former rebel who had become quite weary of all of the fighting at this point was the aforementioned "Pirate Queen," Grace O'Malley. O'Malley was now in her later years and a widow. She was worried about the future of the next generation. Her fears and insecurity led her to break down and write a letter directly to Queen Elizabeth herself.

The letter was written sometime in 1593 and would lead to one of the most epic moments in English and Irish history. Grace O'Malley and Queen Elizabeth actually met in person to discuss the latest turmoil in Ireland. Grace and Queen Elizabeth had several sit-down conversations between June and September of 1593. Much of what they discussed lies in the realm of folklore, but some believe that Elizabeth attempted to offer Grace a title, which Grace refused.

More fighting would erupt in 1594 when an English supply convoy was assaulted by Irish rebels. Some fifty-six English troops were killed in the attack. This marked the start of the Nine Years' War.

Leading the charge against the English during this conflict was a powerful earl of Tyrone named Hugh O'Neill. And yes, he was related to the previous rebel Shane O'Neill. However, Hugh led a very different life than his ill-fated relative. Hugh actually spent much of his early years in England, whereas Shane is said to have never spoken a word of English in his life. Hugh was also a Protestant, whereas Shane O'Neill had been a Catholic through and through.

Hugh, who was considered a friend of Queen Elizabeth, was initially considered a valuable pawn to be used in Irish affairs. When he returned to Ireland to stake his ancestral claim, he was being groomed to be an agent of the English. However, in 1598, he decided to join the ongoing rebellion. That year, he handily defeated an English army at the Battle of Yellow Ford near Armagh.

Queen Elizabeth was greatly disturbed to hear of these tidings and immediately dispatched the earl of Essex to see what was afoot. This ill-fated earl quite literally lost his head and was succeeded by Lord Charles Blount, 8th Baron of Mountjoy, who was deputized to take on the Irish.

Charles Blount went down in infamy for his take-no-prisoners approach and scorched-earth tactics. In his struggle against the Irish rebels, he not only killed people, including men, women, and children, but also their livestock. He butchered cattle in the fields and then made sure to burn down any crops growing on Irish farms. Actions such as these would lead to a "manmade" famine. Countless would perish, and the devastation unleashed in the early 1600s would set the template for future scourges.

Interestingly, the most shocking episode as it pertains to Mountjoy's scorched-earth campaign came from his own personal secretary, Fynes Moryson, who recalled a terrible scene around the Irish town of Newry. According to Moryson, children were seen roasting and eating the flesh of their dead mother. Moryson claims that when these kids were asked why they were doing such a terrible thing, they answered they could not get any other meat. When asked what happened to their cattle, the children matter-of-factly reported, "The Englishmen had taken them away."

It is easy to assume that this account is either false or grossly exaggerated, but since it came from Mountjoy's own secretary, one has to wonder what purpose such a tall tale would serve. Did Mountjoy encourage his secretary to produce these tales because they made him look good? Did he promote these stories because he wanted to shock the Irish? Was he proud to have starved the Irish to cannibalism? Or was the account—as shocking as it is—true? Historians may be divided on this particular point, but the well-documented famines that struck the land are not open for debate.

Queen Elizabeth died in March 1603, with much of the plantation system still very much in flux. Just a few days after her passing, the Nine Years War came to a close with the signing of the Treaty of Mellifont, which granted some religious concessions to Catholics and recognized Hugh O'Neill's and his family's titles and lands in exchange for Hugh and his followers to respect and accept English authority. Interestingly, the Pirate Queen, Grace O'Malley, perished that same year.

The most immediate aftereffect of the Nine Years' War was that many leading figures in previous rebellious strongholds, such as Munster and

Ulster, were missing in action. For instance, on September 4th, 1607, Hugh O'Neill, Earl of Tyrone, as well as Rory O'Donnell, Earl of Tyrconnell, the younger brother of Hugh O'Donnell, hopped on a French freighter and left all of their holdings behind.

Apparently unwilling to withstand the increasing pressure on their domain and perhaps hoping to seek support abroad, they fled to continental Europe. This event was known as "the Flight of the Earls," and it, more than anything else, marked the beginning of a massive rush by the English to claim vacated Irish land. It did not take long for the English to lay claim to the various Irish estates that were up for grabs once the Irish elite had left.

Even though both men—O'Neill and O'Donnell—would ultimately perish as exiles in Rome, their former lands, as well as other confiscated properties, would be the home of brand-new plantations. Large swathes of northern and southern Ireland were open for English settlers willing to stake a claim.

In 1610, new rules were enacted that showed England's true goal: to have English residents outpace the local Irish. King James I and his court hammered out new protocols on how to handle these plantations. The new rules were called Conditions of the Plantation of Ulster.

Although the wording of these new rules mentioned only Ulster, the new laws also applied to Donegal, Tyrone, Derry, Armagh, Fermanagh, and Cavan. A big part of the new measures involved the concerted effort to make the implantation of English "cultural values" among the native Irish who remained a routine practice. This was perhaps most evident in Derry, where the English thrust was so pronounced that the name was actually changed to "Londonderry" since Londoners were so involved in its transformation. Such things are almost insulting to residents of Derry today, who likely cringe whenever they hear the Anglicized version of their town's name. But as writer and historian John Gibney rightly described it, these undertakings were a case of "social engineering on a massive scale."[4]

King James seized prime real estate in the Ulster counties of Tyrone, Fermanagh, Donegal, Coleraine, Cavan, and Armagh. This land was then sold on the cheap to British settlers who were willing to make the move. Initially, many of these new landlords tried to recruit fellow Protestants to work their estates, but they quickly realized it would be cheaper and more

---

[4] Gibney, John. *A Short History of Ireland: 1500-2000.* 2017.

practical to simply hire the local Catholics who were already there.

However, it was not all bad for the Irish—that is to say, the poor Irish, who did not have much to lose in the first place. Some economic gains were made after 1603 from which the poorer classes of Irish benefited. From the signing of the Treaty of Mellifont all the way to the mid-17th century, great gains were made in textile production and shipbuilding. All of these enterprises resulted in additional new jobs for the lower-class Irish. Shipbuilding, unfortunately, ended up having negative consequences, as it resulted in the rapid deforestation of large sections of Ireland, leading to timber shortages all throughout the 1630s.

The 1630s is an important marker of progress as it pertains to the English plantations in Ireland. According to writer, historian, and Irish guru John Gibney, by this decade, "the new British presence in Ireland was firmly ensconced."[5] The contentious makeup that would long haunt the region had truly taken shape. Rich Protestant landlords literally lorded over the poor Catholics, creating a simmering cauldron of discontent.

It is true that the poor Irish had jobs, laboring away for these affluent transplants, but their own culture was being oppressed at every turn. Yes, it could be said that by this point, Ireland had already been utterly and irrevocably changed. Little did anyone know, however, that the worst was yet to come.

---

[5] Gibney, John. *A Short History of Ireland: 1500-2000.* 2017.

Chapter 6: The Great Famine and Its Consequences

"Why should Ireland be treated as a geographical fragment of England— Ireland is not a geographical fragment, but a nation."

-Charles Stewart Parnell

Life in Ireland had never been easy, but by the 1630s, conditions had become considerably worse. These dire straits would lead to mass migrations. Some Irish would try their luck in continental Europe, but others would find a new escape valve by way of a continent across the Atlantic called North America.

Irish migration to North America can be tracked in several waves, from the 1630s all the way to the great migrations of the 1840s. The Irish presence was well established in North America by the time of the American Revolution of 1775, and perhaps no one supported the establishment of a free and independent United States more than the Irish. This makes sense. Why wouldn't the Irish be eager to support the independence of a land that would win them a secure refuge and be entirely free from the meddling of the British Crown?

The Irish numbered around half a million at the time of the American War of Independence, and a huge percentage of their number fought to free the nascent United States from Britain's grip. After the American Revolutionary War came to a close, the British were aware they had an increasing problem with the Irish, both abroad and at home.

In an attempt to placate the increasingly distressed Irish, as well as to consolidate British authority, the Acts of Union were promoted in 1800. This act established what would be called the United Kingdom of Great Britain.

For those who are unaware, the term "Great Britain" refers to the greater island of Britain, which includes Scotland, Wales, and England. Ireland was lumped in with these three nations to create what was termed a "United Kingdom." Today, the United Kingdom still exists, but it only retains the northernmost portion of Ireland, known, aptly enough, as Northern Ireland. However, back in the year 1800, the Acts of Union included all of Ireland.

The Acts of Union were a complete slap in the face for many Irish since it disbanded the Parliament of Ireland, which had been hosted in Dublin, in favor of Irish representatives making their way to Westminster, England, instead. Others pointed out that not having their own separate institutions was a step toward better equality.

It was also argued that Irish Protestants would benefit because instead of being a minority in what was still a largely Catholic Ireland, they could become part of the majority of this newly united kingdom. They would be a supermajority of Protestants, as it were, since they were being lumped in with all of the other Protestants in England and other parts of the realm. However, many Irish Protestants felt a great deal of resentment at having this new arrangement foisted upon them.

One can only imagine just how disenfranchised the Irish Catholics must have felt. The notion that their homeland was included in a political union from which they themselves were mostly excluded certainly could not have produced any fans of the British Crown. This perceived exclusion would sow the seeds for further violence.

Now, the favored minority of Protestant Ireland, which, in itself, was largely the scions of the plantation era, had to look increasingly to London for support, whereas the excluded Irish Catholics found even more reasons to look away.

The Irish Protestants felt rightfully threatened by the growing animosity of their less fortunate Catholic neighbors. This insecurity led to the formation of the Orange Order, a fraternal organization said to be loosely patterned off of the Freemasons. The Orange Order focused on the brotherhood of Protestants in what Irish historian Paul F. State describes as being "a sectarian alliance that espoused fierce defense of the union."[6] By the 1820s, the Orange Order and their fanatic loyalty to the Union Jack had reached its height.

While the Irish Protestant, land-holding minority rallied around the flag (at least for the most part), the Catholic majority, which comprised some 80 percent of Ireland's population at the time, created their own underground associations. Members of these groups were known as Ribbonmen, and their organizations had names such as Sons of the Shamrock, Society of St. Patrick, and Patriotic Association of the Shamrock. These groups openly antagonized the Orange Order and often spoke of their desire to spill "Orange blood."

Despite the bold threats, the Irish Catholics remained disenfranchised. However, there was a somewhat successful political organization started by an Irish Catholic lawyer by the name of Daniel O'Connell. O'Connell wanted Catholic emancipation. He founded the Catholic Association in 1823 to help him meet his goal.

Portrait of Daniel O'Connell.
https://commons.wikimedia.org/wiki/File:Daniel_O%27Connell_-_Project_Gutenberg_13103.jpg

---

[6] State, F. Paul. A Brief History of Ireland. 2009.

Daniel O'Connell's Catholic Association sought to make use of the global ties that linked Ireland to the seat of the Catholic Church in Rome, as well as capitalize on inroads made in Ireland through the Irish enclaves that linked Irish commerce. O'Connell and his Catholic Association faced pushback, but beyond all odds, he managed to rise above adversity in a tremendous way. He was even elected as a member of Parliament in 1828, representing County Clare.

This was a watershed moment for Irish Catholics everywhere, but even so, most were not faring so well. Many had become farmhands who eked out a living as tenant farmers. They were given a couple of acres, a cabin, perhaps a cow, and a field to grow potatoes, which had become an Irish staple.

By 1830, the potato had become the main source of nourishment for many Irish. The potato replaced fish and even milk, both of which had previously been the bounty of Irish fishermen and dairy farmers. The Irish were relegated to small plots of land, so they grew the potato out of convenience and necessity. Potatoes are a hardy crop that can be grown on small-scale farms, and potatoes are able to provide ample nutrients.

The Irish climate and especially its soil, which leans toward being a bit on the acidic side, proved to be quite conducive for growing this particular crop in the 1800s. However, there were two major problems. Potatoes cannot be stored for prolonged periods of time, and they are susceptible to disease. In the summer of 1845—the fateful year of the first widespread potato famine in Ireland—it seemed that the elements were conspiring to ruin that year's potato crops.

In consideration of the fact that many Irish victims of the potato famine ended up fleeing to the United States, it is with some irony to note that the cause of the Irish potato famine is said to have originated in the United States. It is believed that a rare fungus came from North America and spread, affecting the potato crops in Britain by quickly decimating all of the potatoes it came in contact with. The blighted potatoes were first witnessed in England before the blight spread to Ireland.

The fungus turned leaves and stalks into blackened, crumbly dust. Potato farmers in Ireland tried their best to salvage crops by removing the affected parts of the plant, but they soon learned that if the leaves were black, the potatoes were likely already affected. According to one account, which appeared in a periodical of the day called the *Freeman's Journal*, a farmer had been harvesting a bountiful crop of perfect, healthy potatoes one day, only to find the rest rendered into "filthy, odorous black mush" the next.

Thomas Gallagher famously wrote about the famine in his book *Paddy's Lament.* He described a "sulphureous, sewerlike" odor, which was "carried by the wind from the rotting plants in the first-struck places." Gallagher furthermore asserted that "Farmers who had gone to bed imbued with the image of their lush potato gardens were awakened by this awful smell and by the dogs howling their disapproval of it."

No matter how hungry the Irish might have been, they were not going to scoop up the nasty, mushy, smelly remnants of what used to be a potato and eat it. Thanks to a pesky fungus now known as *Phytophthora infestans,* their potato crop was destroyed. But what exactly were they to do? Without the potatoes, their main source of nourishment was gone.

The suffering was as much psychological as it was physical. As one member of the local clergy who chronicled this suffering stated, "In many places, the wretched people were seated on the fences of their decaying gardens wringing their hands and wailing bitterly the destruction that had left them foodless."[7]

One can only imagine how devastating all of this must have been. For those who staked just about everything on this crop, it must have seemed like the world had come to an end. Many with a more superstitious bent likely associated the famine with some sort of impending Armageddon. Even though the potato famine did not turn out to be a harbinger of a global doomsday, it sure was hell for the Irish.

It is said that the starving masses did their best to survive. Some learned how to improvise by foraging, hunting wild game, and fishing. These means of food acquisition were rife with difficulty and danger for those who were inexperienced in the practice. For example, people who did not know what they were doing could very easily devour poisonous plants or eat diseased meat in their desperate scramble to find sustenance. According to some accounts, there were even instances of cannibalism reported in the counties of Cork, Kerry, Mayo, and Galway.

Many historical narratives give the impression that the British government did nothing to try and help the starving Irish, but this is not true. It could be easily argued that the British officials did not do enough, but it would be inaccurate to say that they did nothing at all.

---

[7] Neville, Peter. *A Traveller's History of Ireland.* 1992.

The British government, under the administration of Prime Minister Robert Peel, was blindsided by the potato blight. It was certainly an unexpected event, and as such, the first order of business for Peel's government was to figure out what had happened. Many cynical and perhaps even prejudiced members of the British government initially wondered about the veracity of all of the Irish woes they were hearing about. The British were fairly far removed from what was going on in Ireland, and it is also worth noting that the British relied on more than one crop for sustenance. So, for them, the notion that the failure of one crop—the potato—could cause such an outbreak of famine among the Irish seemed hard to believe.

Peter Neville, who wrote *A Traveller's History of Ireland,* was quick to point out that the member of Peel's government put in charge of Irish famine relief, Charles Edward Trevelyan, had made prejudicial statements against the Irish, which, according to Neville, seemed to "have a touch of racism about them."[8]

One of Trevelyan's worst remarks was when he declared that "Ireland must be left to the operation of natural causes," as if it were completely natural for all of the Irish to starve to death. Trevelyan did not view the Irish as proper British subjects in need of help but rather as some sort of second-class citizens who deserved their lot in life. He was of the opinion that the famine needed to run its course. There would be no sympathy from him, only absurd theorizing and ice-cold cynicism.

Many others shared the same views as Charles Edward Trevelyan. They simply refused to believe what was happening. Ireland was part of the greatest empire in the world. The more cynically minded wondered if the Irish were somehow exaggerating their plight. There was certainly a temptation to view the Irish as lazy and inept and that they had brought unnecessary problems on themselves and, by extension, the British government.

Peel instituted a fact-finding commission to make an inquiry into the problem. However, this "scientific inquiry" fell far short of science when they began advising the Irish to do ridiculous things, such as punch holes into the ground near their crops in order to "air them out." Airing out fungus-infested potatoes would not do any good.

---

[8] Neville, Peter. *A Traveller's History of Ireland.* 1992.

When it was realized that the Irish were not exaggerating their issues and that the problem was not going to be fixed easily, efforts were made to somehow help those who had lost their crops.

But despite their hardship, Peel was not into free handouts. In fact, Peel wanted them to work! The Peel government sought to alleviate those hit the hardest by putting them into government-sanctioned workhouses, where the Irish were made to work for their food in terrible conditions.

The workhouses were awful, but for someone starving, it was likely better than nothing. But as the crops continued to fail and the Irish continued to seek relief, it was clear that there simply was not enough room in the workhouses for all of those in need of help.

Fearing that the whole system of relief would collapse, British administrators bought surplus corn from the United States in an effort to provide some form of sustenance to the starving Irish. The government also set up a relief commission to better streamline the doling out of aid.

Most of the Irish had never even seen corn, let alone eaten it. The foodstuff was sold as cornmeal, and many Irish mills were not even equipped to make it. There was a lot of confusion about the new crop, but the Irish took what they could to survive.

Along with corn, money was allocated for a relief fund. Queen Victoria was a generous giver to this relief fund. Of course, the more cynical would rightly point out that she was the queen. If the queen of England could not raise money for the suffering Irish, who were members of the British Empire, then who could?

Interestingly, during this period, the famed American abolitionist Frederick Douglass paid a visit to Ireland. He was absolutely shocked at what he saw. He even informed his compatriot and abolitionist peer William Loyd Garrison that the suffering of the Irish was beyond belief.

Many international charities attempted to help the Irish. One of the famous relief efforts came from the Choctaw tribe in the United States. Having heard of the plight, the Choctaw raised money and sent over five thousand dollars in today's money to the Irish.

Although the Irish suffered greatly, the initial efforts made by the British government to stave off calamity were marginally successful. It might have seemed that Britain had dodged a bullet. However, the famine was not over yet. And when the potato-ravaging fungus returned in 1846, matters became much worse. This time around, the destruction of potato farms was even more widespread.

It seems that the first round of the blight had left spores on the ground, which, due to a wet and rainy season, were submerged deep in the soil. These spores developed a lethal strain of fungus that would overwhelm all of Ireland's potato crops.

Perhaps even worse for the Irish was the fact that the previous prime minister, Robert Peel, and his Tories had been dismissed. The Whigs led by Lord John Russell had taken over the administration.

Russell seemed to lack an understanding of how to deal with the growing crisis and mostly tried a hands-off approach, insisting that local organizations in Ireland should handle the problem. This was no help at all. The British government declared the famine was over in 1847, but the Irish felt the effects of the famine well into 1852.

Many Irish felt they had no choice but to leave their country or starve to death. A mass migration began. Just prior to the famine, Ireland had a population of around eight million. It has been estimated that approximately one million died during the famine. Another million left the country, meaning Ireland lost a quarter of its population in about six years. Irish from all corners of the country made their way to Dublin and other port cities and left on whatever ships they could find with whatever belongings they could carry.

The odds of survival on some of these ships were quite low. The ships became known as "coffin ships." During one voyage to Canada, hundreds perished.

Nevertheless, the Irish continued to flee, with over two million fleeing the country in total. Many headed to Canada or the United States. This number of migrants constituted a stunning quarter of the whole population of Ireland at the time.

The Irish potato famine not only killed a sizeable fraction of the Irish population and led to massive migration abroad, but it also crystallized a strong sense of renewed nationalism among many of the Irish. The Irish who survived this turmoil were hardened and more determined than ever before to rise up and stand for their rights.

Chapter 7: The Easter Rising: The Birth of Republicanism

"We don't believe that winning elections and winning any amount of votes will win freedom in Ireland. At the end of the day, it will be the cutting edge of the IRA which will bring freedom."

-Martin McGuinness

After the incredibly devastating potato famine, those who remained in Ireland began to seriously consider independence. It was clear that the British administration was not working, and for many, the potato famine was literally a do-or-die moment. So, the Irish called upon the greatness of their ancestors and tried to martial their warrior spirit to fix their plight.

In 1858, Irish political activist James Stephens launched the Fenian movement. This political movement was named after the Irish soldiers of the past, the Fianna. As historian Paul F. State puts it, "A secret fraternal society, the Fenians (the name alludes to the Fianna army of ancient Irish mythology), was founded in Dublin in March 1858 and in New York City in April 1859, although it may have had informal beginnings a decade earlier in Ireland."[9]

It was not long before this militant group took action. In 1867, matters came to a head when high-ranking members of the Fenian movement were executed after some of their members launched an assault on the police.

---

[9] State, F. Paul. A Brief History of Ireland. 2009.

The following year, Britain elected a Liberal prime minister, William E. Gladstone. Prime Minister Gladstone would be important in the events of Irish independence. Although he could not quite be characterized as being sympathetic with all of the ambitions of the Irish, he was pragmatic enough to understand an untenable situation when he saw one. Prime Minister Gladstone made some of the first major moves to actually do something about the Irish.

The idea of home rule began to be discussed more and more. The notion of home rule was not calling for a complete break from the British Empire or the United Kingdom; instead, the people who were part of the Home Rule movement wanted the establishment of a separate parliament in Ireland so the Irish could have some say in how their affairs were governed.

Essentially, instead of having every rule dictated to them from London, England, Home Rule advocates were demanding that rulings be made in Dublin, Ireland. All rulings would still have to be approved by higher authorities in the United Kingdom, but direct representation from Ireland would be an integral part of the process.

This was especially important for the landed elite of Ireland since they were the ones who often had to carry the heavy burden of dealing with the poor, starving masses during the potato famine. Many of the better-off Irish landlords had been placed in a truly unenviable position since they were expected to cobble together charitable efforts on the ground without enough help from the politicians in London. Such things served as a glaring indication that Ireland needed some sense of home rule in order to be able to handle some of their problems on their own.

Whether they admitted it or not, there were many in London who could not help but agree due to the mismanagement disaster that had occurred during the potato famine. Not all would openly admit that out loud, of course, out of fear of alienating their English constituents, but they likely saw the writing on the wall all the same.

Under the administration of Prime Minister William Gladstone, the British Parliament implemented the Land Act on August 1ˢᵗ, 1870. This bit of legislation is considered to be the first effort by the British government to truly address the plight of tenant farmers in Ireland.

Seeking to unwind some of the restrictions that had chained the Irish to the land on which they worked, the Land Act gave them basic rights and also promised to hold the landlords accountable if they suddenly decided to evict their tenants for no good reason.

That same year, an Irish politician named Isaac Butt began to advance the cause of home rule and the call for Ireland to have its own separate parliament. Butt's group became known as the Home Rule League, which managed to pick up several seats in the 1874 general election.

These efforts sought to achieve through legislation what countless Irish warlords could never do by force—they sought to bring some sense of homegrown authority back to the Irish homeland.

The Irish found an unlikely champion in Charles Stewart Parnell. Parnell was a land-holding Irish Protestant, but he had his reasons for struggling for the cause of home rule. Parnell's Home Rule Party (also referred to as the Home Rule League) consisted primarily of the tenant farmers who had lost so much during the potato famine. Parnell and his championship of home rule coincided with the rise of the aforementioned Prime Minister William Gladstone.

Gladstone was a liberal politician who took a much more conciliatory position on Ireland than many of his peers at the time. Gladstone made several efforts to push through legislation that would allow Ireland to have greater autonomy. However, these efforts, which were highly unpopular in England, continued to fail.

Even so, the Liberals found themselves in a box. They could not get a majority to support the agenda of home rule, but they also could not afford to lose the sizeable fraction of Irish members of Parliament who supported it.

The conservatives in Britain found it profitable at the ballot box to swing in the complete opposite direction, so Britain became split between one side that was vehemently against home rule and another that was tacitly trying to support it.

Matters became even worse when violent attacks ensued, which were perpetuated by Irish radicals. One of the most infamous was the Phoenix Park Murders, which occurred in Dublin on May 6th, 1882. Some of the targets in this deadly attack included none other than the newly made chief secretary of Ireland, Lord Frederick Cavendish, and his undersecretary, Thomas Henry Burke.

Having a chief secretary appointed by London was anathema to those who supported home rule. However, for the most part, even the staunchest home rule advocates greeted the news of this atrocity with horror.

Nevertheless, the march toward home rule continued. Even after the death of Parnell in 1891, many of his ideas continued to live on through his supporters. Irish politician John Redmond, in particular, sought to carry forward Parnell's legacy by openly calling for not just home rule but a fully independent Irish republic.

Around this time, another prolific political figure emerged on the Irish landscape: Arthur Griffith. Griffith agreed with many that the Acts of Union passed in 1800 were illegal. Many Irish believed that since no one had consulted the Irish if they wanted to be lumped in with Great Britain that the law should not stand as written.

However, rather than focus his efforts on using parliamentary measures to diminish or even repeal the Acts of Union, Griffith insisted that since the law was illegal and illegitimate, the best thing to do would be to flat-out ignore it. He urged Irish members of Parliament to skip out on British Parliament altogether, instead stating that all Irish elected officials should meet in a local legislative body made up of just Irish representatives. There, they could hash out how to rule Ireland among themselves without any say from England.

Griffith's focus on creating an all Irish legislative body that could shut out the English led to the creation of a political party known as Sinn Fein, which actually translates as "We Ourselves." This party was created in 1905.

The divisive nature of Irish/British relations would continue to simmer until it truly came to a boil when World War One broke out. The extra stress and burden of the First World War truly broke the camel's back as it pertained to the question of home rule for Ireland.

In 1914, Ireland found itself in an interesting position. The world was at war, but the notion of a draft was not popular with the Irish public. Even so, during the course of the conflict, some 200,000 Irish troops would serve in the war, and some 35,000 would be killed. These Irish troops served with distinction during the Gallipoli campaign, which saw British troops stuck in a quagmire in Turkish terrain in the early stages of the war.

Back in Ireland, a vociferous call for home rule had once again ensued. Legislation to allow some semblance of home rule to take shape was established on September 18th, 1914, but it was decided that any further enactment of it would be put off until the war had concluded.

However, that was not enough for many Irish activists. In the middle of the war, on April 24th, 1916 (Easter Monday), a group of radicals seized government facilities in Dublin and called for Irish independence. This uprising of Irish nationalists would go down in history as the Easter Rising.

England responded by declaring martial law the day after the uprising began. Over the next few days, tens of thousands of British troops swarmed in and sought to destabilize a growing—and considering the state of wartime Britain—very much unwanted crisis. A state of war between England and Ireland existed. British troops set up artillery and pounded the locations where the Irish rebels were holed up. The rebels ended up surrendering on April 29th, having to deal with a large number of casualties. After some six days, the crisis was over, with hundreds dead, thousands wounded, and most of Dublin destroyed.

It is surprising how little this footnote of World War One is mentioned, but Britain essentially had to fight a brief war in its own backyard while their troops were embroiled in the trenches. It certainly was not a good feeling for anyone involved. Matters would become even worse when the victorious English decided it would be a good idea to execute many of the prisoners.

Despite the trouble caused by the Irish militants, this incident created a lot of sympathy for the Irish plight. An Irish member of Parliament named John Dillon gave a famous speech on May 11th condemning the action. Dillon stated, "It is not murderers who are being executed; it is insurgents who have fought a clean fight, however misguided, and it would be a damned good thing for you if your soldiers were able to put up as good a fight as did these men in Dublin."[10]

The immediate aftermath of the debacle also managed to shine more light on the Irish organization called Sinn Fein. Although a fringe group, Sinn Fein gained attention for supporting the Easter Rising. After the uprising, almost all of the radicals—whether it was true or not—were lumped into the Sinn Fein category. Interestingly enough, Arthur Griffith, the founder of the Sinn Fein Party, would be arrested in the immediate aftermath of the Easter Rising, even though there was nothing (besides perhaps his political rhetoric) directly connecting him to the insurrection.

Further developments in 1918 would lead to even more drama. After German troops on the Western Front threatened Allied progress, the

---

[10] Gibney, John. *A Short History of Ireland: 1500-2000.* 2017.

British began to institute a draft in Ireland for the first time.

It seemed that the Irish were fine with sending troops in droves when it was on a voluntary basis, but they openly balked at serving in the war when it was deemed to be some sort of fulfillment of a required duty to the United Kingdom.

The Irish, who were still feeling just about as disenfranchised as ever despite any legislative progress that had supposedly been made, could not countenance that they were being forced to fight for a country that they themselves did not feel they were a part of. Many of the more frustrated Irish began to look toward Sinn Fein in earnest. The Irish Volunteers also began to throw their weight behind Sinn Fein, and soon they would come to form what would be dubbed the Irish Republican Army or IRA for short.

The IRA would take on terrorist characteristics. In 1919, a couple of British officials were killed by two radicals named Dan Breen and Sean Treacy, who claimed to be operating under the agency of the Irish Republican Army. By the following year, the IRA and Sinn Fein had become increasingly active.

Rising to lead the movement was an American born, Irish ideologue descended from a Spanish father and an Irish mother. His name was Eamon de Valera.

De Valera was incredibly active during the unrest of 1916. By 1917, he was a leading figure in Sinn Fein, becoming the president. Sinn Fein was positioning itself as a champion for the cause of independence during the postwar era. And sure enough, in the general election of December 1918, Sinn Fein managed to win seventy-three seats in the British Parliament, which was a great achievement for any political party, especially one with as much at stake as Sinn Fein. However, there was much talk of electoral cheating at the time, and even Sinn Fein supporters openly admitted to malfeasance at the ballot box. As it pertains to potential fraud in the 1918 election, writer and historian Peter Neville spoke of the phenomenon of "impersonation."

According to Neville, it was common for Irish political activists to study the electoral register in advance in order to find names of people who had passed away but were still on the voting rolls. People often laugh whenever accusations are floated that the dead may have voted in an election, but according to Peter Neville, this happened in Ireland's 1918 election.

Neville claims that political hacks took down the names of dead people still on the voting rolls and then sent out agents to "impersonate" them. These agents would then vote on behalf of the dead. As Neville put it, "Sinn Feiners were very good at this, and some claimed to have done it six times in 1918. There were even stories about people doing it twenty times!"[11]

These newly elected members ultimately refused to take their seats in Westminster and instead formed a parliament of their own in Dublin. These newly elected representatives would first convene on January 21st, 1919. On that same day, they declared Irish independence.

Like it or not, Sinn Fein had become a bulwark of opposition against those who did not wish to cut Ireland loose. By 1920, Sinn Fein was in control of the Irish government, controlling most of the local apparatus. Despite claims of election fraud, Sinn Fein seemed to have been supported by most of the Irish people.

The British authorities tried to strike back by unleashing a torrent of what has been described as draconian legislation. This included the formation of a paramilitary unit called the Black and Tans, whose members wore a hodgepodge of police and military ("black and tan") gear. These troops roamed the streets attempting to enforce the state of martial law that much of Ireland had been placed under. As one can imagine, having an occupying force on Irish soil did nothing to make the Irish think any fonder of the British Crown.

On the contrary, the Black and Tans bullied and attacked Irish civilians for something as small as violating curfew. Homes and businesses were burned, and people were killed or injured. Sinn Fein continued to stoke the outrage from the seats of their shadow parliament assembly, which convened in violation of British law.

It should not be too surprising to hear that Sinn Fein would attempt to create its own legislative body with the Irish as representatives since Sinn Fein means "We Ourselves." Proponents of Sinn Fein furthermore viewed the British takeover during the Acts of Union as illegal. Therefore, British authority in Ireland was not legitimate. As much as the British cried foul, Sinn Fein insisted that it was the British who were violating the rights of the Irish.

---

[11] Neville, Peter. *A Traveller's History of Ireland.* 1992.

In many ways, the British troops sent to Ireland were fighting a losing battle from the very beginning. First and foremost, the British troops were viewed as an occupying force, and the Irish rebels were viewed as freedom fighters. The British soldiers were in hostile territory, being thwarted at every step, while their antagonists were on friendly home terrain in which they could easily disperse, hide, and gain support before coordinating their next strike.

Many often cite America's war in Vietnam as an unpopular one, in which the Americans fought not only an official army but also the sentiment of the Vietnamese people who wished to drive them out. But this is only half-true. Yes, some Vietnamese villagers sided with the communists, but not all of them. US troops still had most of South Vietnam ostensibly on their side as they fought the communist forces of North Vietnam. However, the British in Ireland, besides a smattering of Protestants around Dublin, were largely outnumbered and surrounded by Irish Catholics who were hostile to their presence in the region.

Making matters worse was the fact that the British occupying forces came to regard the average citizen as "the enemy." Neither the British troops, whose job it was to patrol Irish streets, nor Irish citizens felt safe. Irish families lived in fear of that "midnight knock" on their door by British soldiers searching for weapons or IRA operatives.

The attempt of the Irish to shake loose of Britain's increasingly harsh grip would be fought until 1921. At the end of this war, the Ango-Irish Treaty (not to be confused with another later treaty of the same name) was put forth. This treaty sought to establish Ireland as a free state and a dominion inside what was known as the British Commonwealth.

The Irish Free State came into effect on December 6th, 1921. The state that came into being was not a republic but a constitutional monarchy with elected representatives in the British Parliament. With this dominion status, the Irish Free State had general independence in governing its own affairs, but the British monarchy remained the ultimate executive authority.

This meant Ireland would be very similar to Canada, which was another British dominion that had gradually worked its way toward independence. However, the Irish were not content. Soon after the treaty for a free state went into effect, two factions of the Irish began fighting each other over their interpretations of what independence really meant.

The Irish Civil War started in Dublin, and it was fought between those who supported the treaty and the anti-treaty IRA. This war would be waged during 1922 and 1923.

The first phase had the anti-Treatyites (the IRA), who were led by Rory O'Connor, take control of the Four Courts. The building was then besieged by the Free Staters led by Michael Collins. Collins's group waylaid the anti-Treatyites with heavy artillery, pushing them out.

There were more anti-Treatyite forces in Cork, but the Free Staters successfully sent forces by sea to confront them. The Free Staters would triumph but at the cost of many lives, including the life of thirty-two-year-old Michael Collins. Collins was gunned down by a group of disgruntled anti-Treatyites in August 1922.

The Irish Civil War fizzled out in early 1923, and the Free Staters were seen as the victors. With de Valera at its head, the Free State of Ireland had been created.

There was a very big catch in all of this because not all of Ireland was given this free-state status. The northeastern corner of the island, which had been the most thoroughly subjected to plantations and all of the other efforts of Anglicization and Protestant proselytizing, would remain linked to the rest of the United Kingdom. The Protestant majority of Northern Ireland wished this to be the case, though.

In 1973, a referendum was held to see whether the majority of people approved leaving the United Kingdom and joining the Republic of Ireland. The vote was boycotted by nationalists, which led to Northern Ireland staying in the United Kingdom.

Map of Ireland today.
https://commons.wikimedia.org/wiki/File:Ei-map.svg

Northern Ireland would remain a lasting sore spot and point of contention for everyone involved. The continued perceived disenfranchisement of Catholics by the Protestants would only make their disapproval more glaring.

It had been a long, hard fight for freedom, but little did anyone know the troubles that awaited the Irish in the years ahead.

Chapter 8: The Troubles: A Turbulent Relationship

"They won't break me because the desire for freedom, and the freedom of the Irish people, is in my heart. The day will dawn when all the people of Ireland will have the desire for freedom to show. It is then that we will see the rising of the moon."

-Bobby Sands

There is a tendency in histories about Ireland to move straight from independence and the end of the Irish Civil War in 1923 to the time of the "Troubles," which began in the 1960s. Although these are two high-water marks in Irish history, there is obviously much that went on between those two historical markers. So, having said that, it would do us some good to go over them briefly.

Immediately after Irish independence was achieved, the most important thing for the Irish was to make sure they were able to maintain a solid economic footing. This would become quite difficult after the stock market crash of 1929. Although this event began in the United States, the crash would send shockwaves all over the world.

The Great Depression, as it would be called, would sink its teeth deep into Ireland by the 1930s, but it would be Northern Ireland that faced the full brunt of this economic devastation. Not since the days of the potato famine were times that tough. And since England had been thoroughly lambasted for supposedly not stewarding the Irish through such calamities before, it became doubly important for homegrown Irish administrators to find successful ways to weather their nation through the storm.

One of the biggest hurdles was simply finding jobs for everyone. By the 1930s, six counties of Ireland were being greatly impacted by unemployment, which was around 25 percent.

One may think that such suffering could bring unity to Ireland through the shared experience of universal hardship. However, as it pertained to Irish Catholics and Irish Protestants, this was not the case. Although the people in Ireland were glad to be free and independent, most still carried some form of an ancestral grudge against "the other."

This could be seen in the 1930s when a disturbance was created by an Irish Catholic gardener who worked at the Parliament compound at Stormont and was fired simply because of his own background. The man was a good worker and a veteran of World War One. He had served with distinction. But for those who despised his faith and saw everything through a jaded sectarian lens, such things did not seem to matter.

In the midst of this increasingly volatile situation, the Free State of Ireland forged a new constitution in 1937, which transformed it into the Republic of Ireland. The constitution reaffirmed some basic aspirations of Irish patriots, such as making the Irish tongue the official language of Ireland. Such things were fairly predictable developments.

Less predictable was the fact that this constitution achieved some rather interesting feats of political sleight of hand. For one thing, it actually staked a claim for Ireland controlling all thirty-two counties while admitting the reality that its jurisdiction is only over twenty-six counties. Even so, the wording of the constitution purposefully left the door open for possible future repatriation. This, of course, did not sit well with the Unionists in Northern Ireland.

It was the start of a very turbulent relationship, for lack of better words. In the backdrop of all of this uncertainty, the Second World War erupted. In many ways, the British, in general, and the Irish, in particular, were still getting over the First World War.

In 1939, shortly after Germany's invasion of Poland and the start of the conflict, most Irish had to decide where they stood in the conflagration. They most certainly were not going to take the side of the Germans, but they did not want to be dragged into the conflict by the British either. To most Irish, a stance of neutrality seemed to be the only viable option available.

President de Valera denounced Germany's aggression but also made it clear that Ireland would remain neutral during the conflict. This was not altogether pleasing for Britain, but it was something the British were willing to—at least grudgingly—accept for the time being.

However, being neutral created its own set of problems. If aircraft, for example, were shot down or landed in Ireland, what were the Irish to do? The question of what to do with prisoners of war showed who Ireland was truly aligned with. If any Germans crash-landed in Ireland, they were interned, while Allied service members who landed were quietly transported to England.

Northern Ireland, however, was another matter entirely. Since Northern Ireland was part of the United Kingdom, it was an active participant in the war. Northern Ireland ended up being a staging ground for arriving American troops. A large number of US troops were stationed there during the war.

Interestingly, Northern Ireland made the most progress from an economic standpoint after the war. From 1945 to 1968, Northern Ireland made vast improvements in monetizing assets from agriculture and livestock. Northern Ireland went through a veritable export boom, in which livestock and other agricultural products were shipped to the rest of Great Britain.

Even so, unemployment was still a fairly heavy burden to bear, and it was the Irish Catholics who bore the brunt of it. Historians believe many of these issues were not done intentionally, but the downtrodden of Northern Ireland saw things differently. These hardships were often viewed as being part of a concerted larger plot to actively oppress Irish Catholics.

In this tense backdrop of suspicion, decisions that might have seemed rather innocuous at first glance, such as placing a new university in the Protestant town of Coleraine rather than Catholic Londonderry (or Derry), took on a whole new meaning. In light of these growing misgivings, support for the IRA in Northern Ireland began to pick up speed.

As hostilities began to boil over, Northern Ireland, in particular, began to enter a period widely known as the Troubles. This turbulent period, which spanned from the 1960s to the 1990s, would see instability, strife, turmoil, and bloodshed as the Irish in Northern Ireland struggled to find their footing and their identity.

Contrary to popular opinion, not all of the Irish in the north who were seeking change wanted to make progress through bloodshed or the use of force. In the 1960s, there was a growing nonviolent civil rights movement in Northern Ireland. This organization was known as the Northern Ireland Civil Rights Association (NICRA), and much of the rhetoric and strategies of this movement were patterned off of the American civil rights movement.

The group was founded in February 1967. There were many parallels between the NICRA and America's civil rights movement, but one of the most disturbing was how both groups were often met with violent police action.

On October 5th, 1968, for example, several marchers were stopped as they tried to pass through Londonderry (also known as Derry). These peaceful demonstrators were smashed into by the Royal Ulster Constabulary (RUC). The RUC was the designated police force of Northern Ireland, which was almost entirely Protestant in its makeup.

At this point in time, there were many Catholics in Northern Ireland who believed that the only solution was to separate from the United Kingdom outright. The largely Protestant majority who disagreed wanted to stay and were known as "Unionists."

This contentious situation came to a head in the summer of 1969. That August, the Unionists launched a series of vicious assaults on Catholic neighborhoods in Belfast and Londonderry. The situation seemed dire, and all eyes were on the leadership (or lack thereof) of the Unionists of Northern Ireland, led by North Ireland's prime minister, James Chichester-Clark.

When local governance did not seem to be up to the challenge of keeping the peace, British troops began to show up in force. It was not long before the heavy-handed tactics of the British army inflamed sentiments in Northern Ireland.

First, a harsh curfew was put in place in July 1970. This was not popular with anyone, and the harsh manner in which it was enforced was only bound to cause trouble. Something even worse happened the following summer, in August of 1971. Irish Catholic neighborhoods were targeted for internment. Much of Northern Ireland exploded in violent riots. During a particularly bad spate of rioting, twenty-two people died, and countless others were forced out of their neighborhoods due to the wanton destruction that had ensued.

It was around this point that the IRA (Irish Republican Army) is said to have been revitalized. The IRA was increasingly seen by many Irish Catholics as not a radical group but the actual guardians and protectors of the Irish Catholic way of life. Essentially, the only thing standing between the Irish Catholics and certain destruction at the hands of the Unionists and the British army was the IRA.

The IRA had two ideological wings, one that leaned left and one that leaned right. These two wings first crystallized on January 11th, 1970, during a Dublin meeting of IRA representatives when the Official IRA decided to continue the struggle through political means. The more radical right-wing group known as the Provisional IRA splintered off and set itself on a much more militant and confrontational path.

This group called themselves "Provisional" in reference to the Provisional Government of Dublin, which had gone into effect in 1916. The Provisionals (often referred to in slang as "Provos") accused the Official IRA of being leftist and even Marxist in character. But most importantly, the Provos disagreed with the Official IRA's nonviolent stance.

The Provisional IRA believed they were well past the time for talk and deliberation and that force was indeed necessary. This confrontational approach was on full display in the spring of 1970. In remembrance of the Easter Rising that had occurred several decades prior, violent demonstrations were held by the Provisional IRA.

The use of heavy-handed tactics by the British during the unrest of 1971, most especially the internment of Irish Catholics, played into the hands of IRA belligerents of all stripes. The British had provided Irish Catholics all the reason in the world to look up to the Provisional IRA for support. The Provisional IRA (sometimes referred to as Provos) declared that the only solution to the problems facing Northern Ireland was to sever ties with the United Kingdom.

The Unionist Protestants of Northern Ireland, of course, did not agree, so the dilemma continued. This dilemma reared its ugly head in a terrible way in 1972 when a group of British paratroops massacred a group of thirteen Irish Catholic civil rights advocates in Londonderry. This incident, known as Bloody Sunday, would firmly put the Irish Catholics on the side of the IRA.

The Official IRA would soon take action as well, with several coordinated attacks being launched on British targets. It would later be learned that the IRA entered into a bargain with none other than Libyan dictator Muammar Gaddafi in 1972. Gaddafi, who at one time aided a multitude of militants all over the globe, decided it was in his interest to aid the IRA to provoke the British.

By now, the Troubles were in full swing. Right on the heels of the events of Bloody Sunday, the parliamentary doors of Northern Ireland were closed. In its place, a new agreement was hashed out that would have both Protestant and Catholic representatives engage in a power-sharing arrangement in the form of a consensus government. However, this arrangement strongly favored the Protestants in Dublin and was soon denounced by Irish Catholics.

Ultimately, the Official IRA managed to come to terms, and a ceasefire was eventually arranged in 1972. The Provisional IRA would keep on fighting.

The Provisional IRA revved up its attacks and soon would even reach into England. In 1974, IRA militants targeted and attacked Birmingham. These actions had some calling British Birmingham "British Bombingham."

Ireland was going through a terrible inflation crisis during part of this period. Much of this was kicked off by the oil embargo of 1973, which led to inflated oil prices in much of the world. As is so often the case, when the price of oil and gas went up, so did the price of food, which had to be transported by trucks that were suffering at the pump over the inflated gas prices.

There was a decisive uptick in violence during this time. Between 1973 and 1976, random people were killed, and buildings were demolished in terrorist attacks. A series of bombings reached all the way into England itself, gaining much attention in 1973. Furthermore, it is said that over two hundred people were killed on average each year thereafter, with the most being killed in 1976. In 1976, a whopping 297 were killed as a result of the political upheaval in Northern Ireland.

That fateful year of 1976 saw the IRA massacre ten random Protestants in revenge for six Irish Catholics who had been previously killed. This bloody incident, known as the Kingsmill massacre, was soon followed by an event that managed to get even more attention. A UK ambassador, along with a fellow civil servant, were blown up after crossing a landmine in Dublin.

However, the most damning incident happened in August of that year when a supposed IRA Provo militant was shot by British troops during a high-speed chase. The militant ended up crashing his stolen vehicle and killing a few kids in Belfast. This sad incident led Mairead Corrigan, the aunt of one of the kids who were killed, to team up with fellow activist Betty Williams to lead a massive peace demonstration. They demanded all sides put a stop to the violence.

The most important political gesture during this period was the end of the highly controversial practice of internment. However, the end of internment also brought about the end of the United Kingdom viewing those who remained in custody as political prisoners. Instead, they were viewed as just regular run-of-the-mill criminals guilty of crimes against the state. This move was highly criticized by IRA supporters since it meant they would lose many rights and distinctions they had previously held under the designation of political prisoners.

This led to vehement protests by Irish prisoners being held in UK custody throughout the rest of the 1970s and into the early 1980s. The protests began in a rather simple but straightforward manner. The prisoners initially refused to wear the clothes given to them that signaled they were normal prisoners. Instead, these prisoners of war wrapped blankets around themselves while shrugging off any official prison uniforms they were given.

When this failed to get the desired results, they increased their pressure campaign by refusing to get out of their cells. They would not even leave to use the bathroom. Feces and urine soon covered their living space. This rather nasty episode became known as the "dirty protest." This form of protest did get attention, but it did not get the desired result of having the prisoners recognized as political detainees.

By 1980, the prisoners had changed tactics and had decided to embark upon a general hunger strike instead. The group was quite serious about it and refused to give up until their demands were met.

One young man who was part of the hunger strike proved just how serious he was when he literally starved himself to death. That young man was named Bobby Sands, and he would go down as a martyr for the cause of the IRA.

Making matters more interesting, right before Bobby Sands perished, he was actually elected as a member of Parliament. This meant that British Prime Minister Margaret Thatcher had basically refused to give any ground whatsoever to the Irish prisoners, even though one was a member of Parliament.

Thatcher could have cared less if he was a member of Parliament. In her mind, he was a criminal terrorist, and she would not budge one inch to terrorist demands.

In her way of thinking, if Bobby starved, it was his own fault. All he had to do was eat; she was not stopping him from doing so. Even so, many began to view Thatcher as nothing short of a monster for her hardline stance and for not at least attempting to somehow placate the starving twenty-seven-year-old enough to convince him to give up the hunger strike.

The IRA only grew stronger as a result. The propaganda coup brought about by the uncaring prime minister who "let Bobby starve" was great for recruitment.

Sinn Fein once again rose to prominence as well, this time as a well-oiled political machine. The main gears of this machine were IRA stalwarts Gerry Adams, Martin McGuinness, and Danny Morrison. The mobilization of Sinn Fein proved successful and gained results. This was evident in the election that took place in the fall of 1982, which saw Sinn Fein gaining a full 10 percent of the votes cast. The following year, Gerry Adams secured a seat in Parliament.

But even as some IRA members were seeking results through the ballot box, others were sticking to bullets. In 1979, eighteen British troops were massacred at Warrenpoint. This was followed by the assassination of Louis Mountbatten, 1ˢᵗ Earl of Mountbatten, who was a relative of the British royal family. He was killed while in Ireland during the holidays.

The early 1980s were full of violent acts. In 1984, for example, the IRA bombed a hotel where the Conservatives, including Margaret Thatcher, were meeting. Thatcher just barely managed to escape unscathed.

This stunning incident made it abundantly clear that something had to be done to stop all of this terror and bloodshed. The Anglo-Irish Agreement went into effect on November 15ᵗʰ, 1985, with the official backing of both London and Dublin in an effort to solve the problem of Northern Ireland.

Violence would continue over the next few years. Eleven Protestants were killed during a bloody incident in 1987, and a whopping twenty-seven were murdered in 1993. But even so, efforts were made by both Dublin and London to find a solution. This road map would continue to be followed throughout the 1990s.

The Downing Street Declaration was made in 1993. Overseen by Prime Minister John Major, this declaration stated that the United Kingdom no longer had any real strategic interest in Northern Ireland.

It was further stated that if a majority of those who lived in Northern Ireland voiced an interest in returning to Ireland, the United Kingdom would not stand in their way. This mutual agreement helped lead to an official ceasefire between the Provisional Irish Republican Army and the government of the United Kingdom on August 31st, 1994.

Aiding the process was the establishment of the Forum for Peace and Reconciliation, which was put in place by government officials in Dublin in October 1994. This special venue created a platform in which opposing sides could talk and openly air their grievances without any fear of violence or retaliation.

These peaceful overtures would face turbulence in the spring of 1996 when radical factions within the IRA grew impatient with the process. There was also growing fury at the trespasses of an increasingly belligerent Orange Order. As mentioned earlier in this book, the Orange Order is a fraternal Protestant organization.

Irish Protestants were literally on the march in 1996, marching in extravagant parades to show their support for Protestantism and unionism, to the chagrin of local Catholics. When they passed through predominantly Catholic neighborhoods, riots erupted. Local governments felt hamstrung to stop the tumult since the Orangemen (as they were called) insisted that it was their right to march. If the government banned the marches, Irish Protestants would run riot.

In the midst of this tumult and unrest, the IRA decided to strike. On February 9th, 1996, these radical militants detonated an explosive device at London's Canary Wharf.

Many had lost faith in Prime Minister Major's efforts by this point, and the following year, 1997, he was voted out in favor of Prime Minister Tony Blair.

Blair seemed determined to patch up the ongoing peace talks. He reached out to his Irish counterpart, Bertie Ahern, and even solicited the aid of United States President Bill Clinton as he attempted to revive the peace talks that had seemingly stalled.

These efforts paid off when another ceasefire was obtained in late 1997, and talks began anew by early 1998. The talks led to the Good Friday Agreement (also known as the Belfast Agreement), which took place on April 10th, 1998. This agreement was hailed by all as the greatest attempt yet to create a lasting peace in Northern Ireland. The agreement called for a devolved assembly in Northern Ireland. This devolved assembly would allow the Unionists and Irish nationalists to have a say in their government in what was viewed as a kind of power-sharing agreement.

The agreement furthermore insisted that violence would be firmly rejected by both sides. The peace agreement was signed on Good Friday, and it seemed as if real progress had been made. However, that did not stop some of the most extreme members of the IRA from conducting one final devastating attack. This occurred in August 1998, just a few months after the agreement had been made, when a car bomb was detonated in the markets of Armagh, resulting in the deaths of twenty-nine people.

The power-sharing portion of the agreement in regard to the devolved assembly was actually revoked in the early 2000s, but it was put back in place in April 2007. Since then, violence in Northern Ireland has fortunately become a much rarer event. The Provisional IRA has ceased functioning as a paramilitary group. So, are the troubles over? We can only hope.

Chapter 9: The Celtic Tiger: The Economic Boom and Bust

"What were once only hopes for the future have now come to pass; it is almost exactly 13 years since the overwhelming majority of people in Ireland and Northern Ireland voted in favor of the agreement signed on Good Friday 1998, paving the way for Northern Ireland to become the exciting and inspirational place that it is today."

-Queen Elizabeth II

One of the reasons the peace talks between Ireland and England became more attractive was the fact that there was a sudden uptick in the Irish economy. It was unexpected by most, but by the early 1990s, as moves were being made to start peace talks, the Irish economy had surged with a sudden unexpected boom.

Ireland was even referred to as the "Celtic Tiger" due to its economy's ferocious and unrelenting growth. The term was apparently first used in remarks by industry giant Morgan Stanley. In a 1994 economic report on the region, writer Kevin Gardiner referred to Ireland as a Celtic Tiger in light of its sudden rise. This rise has been compared with the sudden rise of some East Asian states, such as Singapore, Taiwan, and South Korea, all of which were previously referred to as economic "tigers."

This Celtic boom has since been largely attributed to post-Cold War investments by both the United States and the European Union. After the fall of the Soviet Union, the United States seemed poised to be the sole super power on the planet. The United States had the most powerful military and the biggest wallet, and for many, Ireland seemed like prime real estate in which to invest.

The European Union was also quite interested in Ireland since it was a Euro-friendly nation (friendly to both European culture as well as European money) with a ready-made English-speaking workforce that could be tapped for a wide variety of roles. Another incentive for investors was the fact that Ireland boasted a much lower rate for corporate taxes.

For these mega-corporations, Ireland seemed like a great place to buy huge tracts of land and construct factories. Ireland became a manufacturing hub, especially in the emerging tech sector. By 1998, around 40 percent of all of Ireland's exports were involved with computing. Both Dell and Gateway used Ireland as a home base for their operations.

All of these investments in Ireland and its economy led to greatly expanded infrastructure and industry in all sectors. And all of this combined, of course, meant plenty of jobs. Instead of waves of Irish fleeing their home country, expats were now returning. Not only that, people who were not even from Ireland were heading to the island for better opportunities.

Eastern Europeans, especially those from nations that had just joined up or were thinking of joining the European Union, flooded into Ireland. Becoming a desirable destination for one seeking a career was new and uncharted territory for Ireland.

For a while, there was a steady and powerful positive feedback loop in place. Investments allowed for growth in industry, which allowed for jobs, which then gave spending power to the populace, who spent their hard-earned cash at retailers, restaurants, and on real estate. All of this money ultimately circled back to the industries responsible for growth, repeating the cycle all over again.

It sounds all perfectly well and good. So, what happened? Well, since most of the investments in the late 1990s to early 2000s were related to tech industries, Ireland was gravely affected when the dot-com bubble burst.

The bubble was created when the general public became heavily interested in all things tech. Computers were being bought, and the internet was being used by a wide swathe of the public sector for the first time.

The dot-com boom was really no different from many other technology-related booms that have occurred in history. The mass implementation of railroads in the 1840s, for example, had a similar boom, and so did the sudden widespread availability of cars a hundred years later.

Riding these sudden waves of consumer enthusiasm is great while they last, but as it pertains to the dot-com boom, there was a sudden and unexpected slump in the tech industry.

A wide range of theories have been presented as to why this happened, from just general declining interest to companies being way too fearful of the Y2K crisis. Y2K was used to refer to a computer programming shortcut. People feared that the internal clocks in computing systems, which had been originally programmed to run on just two digits to signify the years, would be unable to recognize the year 2000, which, in a two-digit format, would have been reduced to "00."

Whatever the reason, there was a decline in sales, corporations briefly panicked, and the dot-com bubble burst. Thus, investment in Ireland suffered as a result.

Unfortunately for Ireland, the other major moneymaker for the Emerald Isle—tourism—suffered as well after the terrorist attacks on New York City, US, on September 11th, 2001. Because of the attacks, many began to reconsider flying on a plane. The 9/11 attacks saw terrorists slamming commercial planes into New York's World Trade Center, as well as America's military nerve center, the Pentagon. There was a fourth plane, but the hostages on board were able to take it over, crashing the plane into a field in Pennsylvania. No one survived any of the plane crashes. Fear of flying led to a decisive drop in tourism, and Ireland was adversely affected as a result.

Ireland began to somewhat recover by 2003, but there were other problems ahead. Many investors had found that it was much cheaper to take their business to eastern Europe, where the people were not demanding high wages and expensive insurance premiums.

Such decisions would have many corporations pulling stakes out of Ireland and relocating to eastern European countries. Ireland tried to recoup, and some progress was made. Wishful thinkers even began to speak of a potential "Celtic Tiger 2" on the horizon. But then the housing bubble of 2008 burst, and the shockwaves hit Ireland particularly hard.

Ireland had been a big recipient of bank investments into various properties, so once the Irish property bubble burst wide open, Ireland was in dire need of a bailout. A huge amount of GDP (gross domestic product) was used that year to do just that, but the effort led to a terrible recession.

Even so, all of the economic fortunes that Ireland had been subjected to were enough to fundamentally transform key aspects of Ireland and Irish society. The pull toward the European Union, in particular, has had some lasting and perhaps surprising effects. The adoption of the euro as currency has largely been beneficial for Ireland in that it has greatly opened up Irish markets on the world stage.

In order to remain in the European Union, Ireland has to abide by European Union rules, which has led to a transformation of Irish society. Due to European Union, Ireland finally ditched its antiquated practice of having female civil servants dismissed simply because they had gotten married in 1973. This is just one example, but it shows the potential for social change in Ireland due to EU pressure.

Ireland's connections to the Continent allowed the country to quickly become less isolated and much more cosmopolitan in scope. We can only wonder what changes may be in store for Ireland in the very near future.

Chapter 10: Modern Ireland in the 21st Century

"On the island of Ireland, the issue of the border is more than just a practical issue. It is about emotion, history and politics."

-Penny Mordaunt

The next phase in Irish economic history was the Celtic recovery, which some have referred to as nothing short of a Celtic phoenix rising from the ashes. The Celtic recovery was kickstarted in 2014 and, over the last several years, has proceeded at a rather steady clip. Ireland's GDP is said to have risen as much as 7 percent by 2015, and favorable trends continued in subsequent years. Ireland continues to boast a low corporate tax rate and a highly educated populace, which are both conducive to the tech industry. This has led to a resurgence of tech firms in the nation, such as Apple, Facebook, and Google. Even so, this rapid boom has made many wonder if Ireland just might again see a bubble bust.

Probably the biggest and most glaring flaw in Ireland's economy is the fact that it relies so much on the investment of multinational companies. Ireland is basically presenting itself as a good place for foreign investments. But what about homegrown industries?

Instead of American-originated Apple, Google, Microsoft. and Facebook, how about an original Irish invention or two? As long as the big multinational companies do well, the investment is there, and Ireland remains in good shape. But should they pull out, the Celtic phoenix will soon burn up into a heap of ash.

We also must not forget the drama of Brexit. Although the United Kingdom (including Northern Ireland) decided to make its exit from the European Union, Ireland itself did not. Even so, special protocols were put in place, the Northern Ireland Protocol to be exact, that would still allow for European Union free movement and for the European Union Customs Union to be in effect to avoid cumbersome and unnecessary problems in the region. However, Northern Ireland remains cut off from the European Union single market.

The major point of contention during this whole ordeal was due to the fact that the United Kingdom and Ireland did not wish to have a hard border. They did not want a hard line between Northern Ireland and the Irish Republic that would be difficult to cross. If one were to look at any situation in the world in which the region of a country has been partitioned, such as East Germany and West Germany, one would realize why such matters are sensitive.

Yes, Northern Ireland is still considered to be United Kingdom territory, and yes, the United Kingdom left the European Union, but the rest of Ireland is still part of the European Union. No one wished to create more problems than there already was by making Northern Ireland a strange non-European Union enclave on the same island as the Republic of Ireland.

There would be no United Kingdom version of the Berlin Wall to separate the borders of Northern Ireland from the rest of Ireland. Instead, borders would be relaxed, and much of the European Union protocols would be recognized in Northern Ireland, even though the nation was technically no longer in the EU.

Many hoped that the continued influence of the European Union and the relaxed borders would ease tensions between Northern Ireland and Ireland. This makes sense since the goal of the EU is to create a system of unified European states. People from the Republic of Ireland, Germany, and France are all part of the European Union. Their vision is of a united Europe in which past petty border distinctions are dissolved, and all are simply Europeans.

Most people in Northern Ireland supported remaining in the European Union. However, this support cut mainly across sectarian lines between Catholics and Protestants. Around 56 percent of people in Northern Ireland wished to remain part of the EU. But of course, even though most in Northern Ireland wished to remain, their voices were drowned out by the larger majority in the United Kingdom, of which Northern Ireland is still a part.

It is quite interesting to contemplate that the relaxing of borders through the European Union led to the Republic of Ireland and Northern Ireland drawing closer together after years of isolation. In the past, most specifically during the time of the Troubles, one had to go through countless military checkpoints just to cross from Northern Ireland to the rest of the island.

The Good Friday Agreement, which brought an end to the violence, began the process of phasing out this previously hard border, a process that was completed in 2005. With both sides now practicing the soft borders prescribed by the EU (even though Northern Ireland is no longer in the EU as of 2024), it is practically just a walk in the park to get to one side or the other. Local Irish and passport-carrying tourists are very thankful for that.

In consideration of all of this, we can only speculate what things may mean in the days ahead. Can the European Union provide a bridge for Northern Ireland to be repatriated back to full Irish control some point before the close of the 21st century?

Interestingly enough, in April 2017, the European Union actually considered this very thing and decreed that if Northern Ireland ever officially unified with the rest of Ireland, it would automatically be considered part of the EU.

Of course, when the 2020 pandemic hit, things changed drastically. Ireland, however, immediately rose to the challenge. Ireland was consistently ranked as one of the top countries as it pertained to how they managed the crisis, especially when it came to getting the public vaccinated.

Ireland was seen as a world leader for how it handled the pandemic while mitigating potential damage to Irish society and the economy. In 2021, Bloomberg.com recognized Ireland as a leading nation for how it handled the storm. The reasoning behind this ranking is said to be due to the fact that Ireland's vaccination rates were among the highest at the time. In other countries, there was a lot of vaccine skepticism and hesitancy, but in Ireland, it seems that most Irish had no qualms about rolling up their sleeves and getting the vaccine.

Ireland might have been a leader during the pandemic, but the country has always been a bit reluctant to lead others on the international stage.

For instance, Ireland has tended to remain neutral in military conflicts that have entangled many other nations.

Ireland might have sent volunteers to support the British effort during World War One, but as soon as Ireland became a free state, it made it clear that it desired to remain neutral from that day forward. Ireland was famously neutral during World War Two and has mostly remained so in the major conflicts that have sprung up across the globe.

However, the Russian invasion of Ukraine in the spring of 2022 began to make many in Ireland, as well as those who consider themselves to be Ireland's friends, reconsider. Initially, Ireland stuck to the typical playbook, with Irish Prime Minister Micheal Martin declaring that Ireland fully intended to retain its status as a neutral, non-belligerent nation on February 24th, 2022.

He did allow for a small caveat to this. He insisted that although Ireland would not get involved militarily, it could get involved on a political level. As Prime Minister Micheal Martin put it, "Ireland's official policy is to be militarily non-aligned. We are, however, not politically non-aligned."[12] Still, as of this writing, Ireland has stopped short of offering any kind of direct military aid or assistance.

Ireland has reasons for its neutrality. Ireland is a fairly small country, and its alliances are a bit more complicated than most. Ireland is technically aligned with Britain, but Ireland's relationship with Britain has been a historically difficult one. Thus, there still remains a cautious political (as well as emotional) distance between the two.

During World War Two, the Irish faced invoking the wrath of both the British and the Germans if they were to side too closely with either one. Neutrality was decided to be the most practical policy. Of course, one may argue that neutrality is the easy way out and that there could be a day in which Ireland will have to make a choice.

Some wonder if Ireland is on the verge of making that choice in light of Russia's invasion of Ukraine. In many ways, Ukraine and Ireland are very similar nations. Ukraine, just like Ireland, has long been bullied by its more powerful neighbor, Russia.

---

[12] O'Halloran, Marie. "Ireland Is Not Neutral About Ukraine." https://www.irishtimes.com/politics/2022/11/15/ireland-is-not-neutral-about-ukraine-taoiseach-insists-in-renewed-row-over-constitutional-position/.

It will be a bit much to go into the whole history of Russian antagonism against Ukraine, but we can at least trace it back to the days of the Russian Empire when wholesale cultural campaigns were forced upon occupied Ukraine. The Russian tsars tried to force Ukrainians to speak Russian and become "Russified." If this sounds an awful lot like Britain's attempt at social engineering in Ireland by installing plantations, you would be right.

The fact that such a small and typically underestimated country like Ireland has gained such worldwide recognition is indeed remarkable. In light of all of these developments in the 21st century, one can only speculate what the next few decades may bring. It would be interesting to see a fully unified Ireland by the time the 22nd century rolls around. But only time will tell.

Conclusion: The Resilience and Unity of Ireland

To say that Ireland is a tough and resilient nation is perhaps one of the greatest understatements of all time. The fact that Irish culture, Irish language, Irish music, and other customs remain and are celebrated today is a strong testament to the enduring nature of Irish civilization. If one were to look at the history of how England attempted to insert plantations into Ireland to subsume its character and dramatically change the culture of the region, it is indeed impressive that Ireland has remained a unique civilization outside of England.

Ultimately, the most damage that England did as it pertains to Ireland is in regard to Northern Ireland. A strong divide between Protestants and Irish Catholics was created there. However, these differences have eased with the passage of time. Of course, there are tensions, but the violence over religion is not as prevalent today as it was in the past.

Today, Catholics outnumber Protestants in Northern Ireland. The nation is undergoing a transformation in which the damage of enforced Anglicization is being reversed, and all things Irish are being revitalized. It has been said that the best thing that ever happened to the Republic of Ireland and Northern Ireland was their entry into the European Union, and there are a lot of great arguments that can be made to that point.

The European Union has its critics, of course, but if there was ever any country that benefited the most from the sweeping changes that entry into the EU can provide, it was Ireland, most especially Northern Ireland.

Suddenly, it seemed as if Northern Ireland was no longer divided from the rest of the island. Without any official unification, it seemed that at least some sense of unity through the EU had been achieved. And the implications are far-reaching. The culture and politics of the two Irelands are starting to blend. By the early 2020s, Sinn Fein had become popular in Northern Ireland. This would have been unthinkable before, yet now, it has become a reality.

Of course, such tidings are not welcome by all. The Unionists are not pleased with Northern Ireland's increasing political ties with the popular political brands of the Republic of Ireland. Some of the more cynical and critical of British politics may even speculate if the British backed out of the European Union and instigated Brexit because Northern Ireland was becoming too close to the Republic of Ireland.

Could it be that the unifying force of the European Union, which managed to unite the entire island of Ireland in ways that were previously deemed impossible, threatened the British worldview that Northern Ireland would always be separate and distinct from the rest of the Emerald Isle? One can only wonder.

To conclude, the resilience of the Irish people is indeed remarkable. Although the Irish have faced countless hardships, one cannot deny their passion and strength.

Part 2: Irish Mythology

Enthralling Myths, Folktales, and Legends of Gods, Goddesses, and Mythological Creatures of Ancient Ireland

Introduction

As you crack open this book, you're probably considering what the point of learning about old Irish myths might be.

Is it for entertainment? Certainly some of these stories are thrilling, dramatic, and spooky. But there is more to Irish mythology than just the elements of drama and thrill.

If you truly want to learn about Irish culture, mythology is the key to understanding. Mythology is the intellectual framework used by the ancestors of a culture to make sense of the world around them. As these stories are passed down orally from generation to generation they become cemented in the people's culture and traditions, creating a national identity and fueling belief systems.

The cultural values of Ireland are no exception, as they are founded firmly in Irish mythology.

Anyone can flip through a book of "Celtic" tales and pluck out bits and pieces to use as part of a fantasy story, put in a comic, or use for a tattoo. Many Irish people today have a sour taste in their mouths from the use of their cultural identity as cheap entertainment—but not because they dislike sharing their culture and myths. Rather, non-Irish people who use flashy elements from Irish heritage lack a true understanding of the meaning and relevance of Gaelic words and Irish heroes.

This book aims to give readers a thorough introduction to the necessary context for understanding the origins of Irish mythology. The information contained within will help readers explore the meaning of the most popular stories and characters throughout the Four Cycles of Irish

Mythology and have a head start in researching Irish mythology from a cultural perspective.

With this knowledge, readers can avoid using Irish myths as a misunderstood and often disjointed source of easy entertainment and instead truly appreciate the unique and beautiful heritage that Irish myths and folklore bring to Irish culture.

Within this book, you'll read about the creation myths of Irish mythology. You'll learn about the Tuatha Dé Danann, the gods and goddess of early Irish mythology. As we delve into the Four Cycles, you'll hear about the most famous stories and heroes that shaped Irish culture. You'll learn the true history behind main players in Irish mythology like the banshee and the fairy, well known around the world today as cartoon and fantasy figures.

Irish heritage is so much more than a St. Patrick's Day parade and leprechauns. To find a genuine understanding and appreciation for the fantastical tales of Ireland, please put aside everything you've learned about fairy tales and continue reading to find out culturally relevant information about true Irish mythology.

Chapter 1: An Introduction to Irish Mythology

"Many times man lives and dies
Between his two eternities,
That of race and that of soul,
And ancient Ireland knew it all."
- "Under Ben Bulben," W. B. Yeats

Every culture has a set of legends, tales, and mythology that has been passed down from parents to their children over time. Irish mythology is perhaps one of the most famous and well known examples of a shared history because of the way it's seamlessly embedded into both past and present-day Irish culture and heritage.

Irish mythology is a beautiful, poetic, and lyrical interweaving of traditions, myths, culture, and history. The culture of the Irish has been maintained for more than 2,000 years, first with oral tradition and later with words transcribed by religious clerics during the Dark Ages and the medieval period.

Seanchaí is the Gaelic word for Irish storytellers. It's pronounced "shan-a-key." For centuries, the Seanchaí were the keepers of history in Ireland. Similar to bards, they could recite wisdom, lore, and stories from memory. They also traveled from town to town in the same manner as bards, sharing stories and history wherever they went.

The pre-Christian Irish oral tradition preserved by the Seanchaí were shared in a tradition called Béaloideas. Béaloideas refers to all of Irish folklore, including ballads, music, dance, art, and storytelling.

The Celts

But where, you might be wondering, did the myths and legends of the Celts and the Irish originate?

Well, you aren't the only one asking that question. As a matter of fact, the earliest origins of these myths is not one hundred percent certain. What we do know is that the myths were forever preserved in writing by Christian monks who mixed in their morals and beliefs with the pagan magic and mystery contained within Irish folklore.

The first Celts were a group of farmers, tribes, and warriors. They were technically Indo-European people, but we can generally say they came from the Alps region of Europe into Ireland in waves of migration over a period as long as one thousand years.

The exact dates of their arrival aren't known, but it's believed they began arriving around the Late Bronze Age into the Early Iron Age. That would be sometime between 800 to 300 BCE.

The Celts shared a common set of values. They loved storytelling, religion, beauty, war, and being victorious in battle.

The Greeks and Romans thought of the Celts as lower-class primitive people, though they respected the Celts' extreme bravery in battle.

To see the Celts fight was a terrifying site. Celts often fought completely naked or in brightly colored tartan pants, covering their bodies in elaborate painted designs and gluing their hair into tall spikes. They wore long, drooping mustaches. Before the battle started, they would bang their swords on their shields and scream, attempting to scare the enemy into fleeing so that they could then attack.

The Celts spread out over Ireland, dominating the previous inhabitants of the island, and it was here the first myths were born.

These Celts are historically known as the pre-Christian ancient Gaels, or Goidelic-speaking Celts. When the Celtic Gaels arrived in Ireland, they discovered mysterious massive stone structures. These were the dolmens and cairns, along with the earthen burial mounds known as tulumi. The Celts believed the burial mounds were portals to the Celtic underworld, which was the land of the gods.

You may be thinking of the famous stone structure called Stonehenge. While Stonehenge is an example of the huge stones found in the British Isles, it is located in England and considered neither a dolmen or a cairn.

One of the most famous dolmens in Ireland is Poulnabrone Dolmen, a Neolithic monument located in present-day County Clare, Ireland. It consists of two upright portal stones supporting a large, flat horizontal capstone that measures about seven by twelve feet.

Historians estimate this portal tomb was built between 4200 BCE to 2900 BCE, making it one of the oldest megalithic structures Ireland has standing today. Archaeologists aren't certain what the full use of the Poulnabrone Dolmen was, but it appears to have been used as a funeral and burial site. Archaeologists have found human remains and pieces of pottery at the site.

Imagine the awe and wonder the Celts must have felt when they stumbled upon these massive stone monuments. They didn't have anyone to explain who built the stone structures, or why. Can you guess what the Celts did to answer their own questions about the uses and origins of dolmens and cairns?

Yes, they created myths based on the stones. Their beliefs blended into the stories behind the stones and burial mounds, beginning a separation between overall Celtic culture and the Celts in Ireland.

Celtic or Irish?

Do you know the difference between the Irish and the Celts? Are they the same thing? Are the two words interchangeable? The simple answer is both yes and no.

Today, Celtic is a cultural term historically associated with all things Welsh, Scottish, and Irish.

The Celts are also often associated with Brittany, France and Catalonia, Spain. At one point, the Celts were spread all over Europe.

Ireland, on the other hand, is a nation that was born from Celtic culture and developed independently during thousands of years of war as it fought to maintain Irish sovereignty. The Irish people began to differ markedly from the Celts with the introduction of Christianity into Ireland. Today, they maintain a proud cultural heritage filled with unique Irish traditions that are related to their Celtic heritage.

It's safe to say that multiple aspects of the Celts and the Irish overlap, but after years of change, Ireland has become its own distinct branch of

Celtic history, making the terms Celt and Irish not as interchangeable as some may assume.

Therefore, when we talk about mythology, we can say that Irish mythology is a branch of Celtic mythology. They share an origin and similarities, but Irish mythology has branched off, with its own unique set of folklore. The beginnings of Ireland are firmly founded in Celtic culture, so we can learn about the Celts as a basis for the beginnings of the Irish.

And what about the Druids? They were not a separate group of people. Druids were Celtic priests. They were responsible for leading religious rituals and giving prophecy, but they were also educators and judges within Celtic society.

The Celts were a very moralistic society who distinguished right from wrong. They had a polytheistic view, with multiple gods and goddesses, but they ultimately believed each individual was responsible for their own salvation. Differing from Christianity, the Celts believed the gods to be their ancestors rather than their creators.

Celtic people believed that when a person died, they were reborn in the "Otherworld." To give each person a good start in the Otherworld, they would be buried with important items such as jewelry, clothing, weapons, and even food and drink. When a person died in the Otherworld, they would be reborn again on Earth.

Each year on October 31, the Celts celebrate the feast of Samhain, otherwise known as All Souls' Day, or Halloween. This is the day when the veil between the Otherworld and our world is the thinnest. The members of the Otherworld will be visible in this world on that day each year. The dead can come back to haunt the living who have wronged them on Halloween, giving inspiration to the Halloween celebration that takes place yearly in the United States.

The Celts believed strongly in trinities. They lived prior to the development of the Christian Holy Trinity many of us are familiar with, leaving us to wonder if they influenced Christian theology. The Celtics believed each person was divided into a mind, body, and spirit. They believed that the world consisted of earth, sea, and air.

Celtic society was organized by tribes and bound together by common beliefs rather than a centralized government. Following the same pattern of trinities, the Celts had three classes. There was a warrior upper class, headed by a king. The middle class consisted of the Druids, who were the educators, judges, and priests. Everyone else was a commoner, both free men and slaves.

Celtic society was not as patriarchal as its Greek and Roman counterparts. Women were valued in society, given equal votes, and even the power to request divorce from men. Celtic myths and history are filled with powerful women queens, goddesses, and heroines.

The Romans

We all know about the vast and far-reaching Roman Empire and its endless historical conquests to take over more territory. As the Romans spread throughout Europe, they wiped out the Celts on the European continent. It took the Romans over four hundred years to fight back the Celtic tribes in Europe and win the territory. In 390 BCE, the Celts in Europe managed to conquer Rome. They held their position over Rome for seven months before Rome took its city back.

Yet the Celts retained a permanent stronghold in Ireland, virtually untouched by Roman rule. Had the Celts been conquered in Ireland, we wouldn't have the beautiful folklore Ireland is so well known for today.

Why did the Romans take over Britain but spare Ireland from invasion? The answer to that question is surprisingly simple.

The first obstacle the Romans faced was the fearsome North Atlantic and Irish Sea. The oceans surrounding Ireland are unpredictable, at best, and deadly at their worst. The Romans were busy maintaining their foothold on Britain; they didn't have time or manpower to tackle the Irish Sea. Geographic isolation protected Ireland and Scotland from the Romans.

The Celts in Britain put up a strong fight, keeping the Romans busy and possibly discouraging them from fighting the Irish Celts. It turns out Ireland wasn't that valuable to the Roman Empire. Ireland didn't have any lucrative exported goods, and it wasn't a great military stronghold due to difficult navigation through the Irish Sea and North Atlantic.

As a result of these factors, the luck of the Irish prevailed. Ireland remained safe from Roman rule, preserving Celtic traditions and allowing Irish culture to flourish.

Mythology's Role

Irish mythology played an important role in ancient Irish culture. As in any ancient culture, myths served several specific purposes. Primarily, myths were placeholders for things people didn't understand. Myths could be answers to any number of questions, like the cause for lightning, the reason for earthquakes, or even an explanation for a sudden illness.

Myths also answer the question of origin. Where did we come from? How did we get here? Ireland has her own mythic answers to these questions that we will discuss in the next chapter.

Myths that are shared across a culture build a strong cultural identity. When everyone believes the same stores and shares these stories with their children, it builds unity across regions and contributes to a national heritage. Soon, the myths are woven into daily life, becoming a permanent part of the culture.

Ireland faced many wars over the years while trying to gain her independence. Myths prevailed across leadership changes and through famines. They even miraculously survived the introduction of Christianity to Ireland, though not without being slightly altered by monks as they were transferred into written text.

The way myths contributed to the sacredness of the Irish land cannot be understated. Many Irish myths are related to a specific place or landmark. Some are about sacred places, battle sites, or even an apparition of a magical being along a well-known road. The Irish hold their land close to their hearts, and the rich oral history behind these specific geographical myths plays a huge role in those feelings.

The social values of the Irish people also prevailed in myths. Tying into cultural unity, the morals parents taught their children through myths helped keep the moral code strong throughout all of Ireland. Irish myths and folklore remind people of a different way of perceiving life. They represent the intersection between humanity and the divine, bringing to life experiences which were both historical and half imagined.

The Cycles of Irish Mythology

Irish mythology is divided up into four cycles. They are the Mythological Cycle, the Ulster Cycle, the Fenian Cycle, and the Cycle of Kings. We will discuss each cycle in depth in the coming chapters.

A basic Celtic knot.
https://commons.wikimedia.org/wiki/File:Celtic-knot-basic-linear.svg

The Mythological Cycle contains strange and wonderful stories that give details about the gods and god-like people who lived in and invaded Ireland in the era before Christianity arrived. These are the oldest stories, the origin stories, of the people who inhabited Ireland. The Tuatha Dé Danann are heavily featured in the Mythological Cycle. They were a supernatural race who represented the primary deities of pre-Christian Gaelic Ireland.

The Ulster Cycle has stories that take place around the first century CE, near the time of the birth of Christ. These stories are some of the most well known of Irish folklore. During this time, wealth was measured by the number of cattle a person owned. (Vikings hadn't yet brought coins to Ireland.) Cattle raids are featured in these stories since cattle were a symbol of wealth and power.

The *Táin Bó Cúailnge*, which has been described as the Irish *Iliad*, is part of the Ulster Cycle.

The Fenian Cycle, also called the Ossianic Cycle, takes place before the Ulster Cycle and the Cycle of Kings. It mainly details stories about hunters and heroes rather than royalty. Some scholars compare these stories to those of the Knights of the Round Table in British literature.

Our hero in this cycle is Fionn mac Cumhaill and his warriors, the Fenians, who were responsible for guarding the High King of Ireland.

The King Cycle, or Historical Cycle, is the fourth and final cycle of Irish mythology. This cycle details the stories of the kings of Gaelic Ireland. In these stories, Ireland herself is often referred to as a living goddess. This cycle features actual historical people but blurs the lines between true history and myth more than any of the other mythological cycles.

In truth, the cycles are not clean-cut divisions. They're more like a Celtic knot, looping together and weaving in and out of each other. Many stories feature characters that intertwine with other stories. A main character will be a side character in another tale, for example. Despite only the first cycle being named the Mythological Cycle, each cycle is considered mythological.

Themes

You will find several major themes enduring across time and distance through Irish myths. These include the human condition, a common cultural identity as Irish, and the eternal struggle between order and chaos.

Familial bonds and tragedy are one of most tragic recurring themes throughout all Irish mythology. Over and over again relationships between family members are put to the test through mythological circumstances, often with a moral lesson. For example, the harmful effects of jealousy on a family can be explored in the famous Children of Lir story.

The continual cycle of life, death, and rebirth is another common motif to watch for in Irish myths. This is often symbolized by the changing seasons and the way the natural world is continually dying and being reborn. These myths give hope to people in unhappy or difficult circumstances, reminding them that everything is renewed in time and not to give up hope. You will see this depicted in the constantly changing fortunes of the Tuatha Dé Danann.

Heroes and the archetypal hero journey are the third motif frequently found in Irish myths. When you're reading a myth for the first time, look out for a hero who faces a trial brought on by battles with supernatural beings. Often the hero will undergo a personal transformation throughout the story, which is meant to inspire people to have courage, overcome their struggles, and consider challenges as a chance to learn and grow.

Finally, consider the theme of conflict and resolution in these myths. Each conflict requires a resolution. The myths will provide a lesson on negotiation or compromise, and perhaps a wise mediator will appear. These stories teach people to beware of the complexities in relationships and to consider ways to practice conflict resolution and promote peace.

William Butler Yeats, the famous poet, once said, "They have caught the very voice of the people, the very pulse of life, each giving what was most noticed in his day." Irish mythology has captured moments in Irish culture and history and frozen them in time, giving generations of Irish people a united culture of myth and legend.

The British did their best to wipe out Irish culture during the last millennium by enacting laws against the Irish language and the Catholic Church. These harsh laws repressed the sharing of folktales and myths in public, making it more difficult for parents to pass on culture to their children.

Where does that leave us in today's modern society, where the primary form of entertainment comes from TV or the internet?

It seems that the days of bards wandering about Ireland sharing tales have long passed. People no longer sit by the hearthside and share stories. Science has explained away many myths and legends.

Thankfully there has been a resurgence of Irish mythology in modern culture. People are fascinated by the stories of old, by the names of the gods and goddesses, and by the magic contained within the lyrical stories. Irish mythology is referenced in all kinds of unlikely places: in Marvel comics, in the show Game of Thrones, and even in modern fairy tales that give a nod to traditional mythological characters while creating new stories to carry on the traditions.

Irish culture is alive and well today. Irish people are spread all across the world, but they remain united by their love of Irish lore and tradition.

Perhaps the best example of Irish lore uniting the diaspora of displaced Irishmen is the worldwide celebration of St. Patrick's Day. In Ireland, St. Patrick's Day is a national holiday. There are many parades all over the country, with the main one held in Dublin. In the US, St. Patrick's Day is also a nationally celebrated holiday with multiple parades. Children celebrate by wearing Irish green to school. The Chicago River is also dyed green in honor of St. Patrick.

In recent years, international landmarks have also turned green in honor of the holiday. The Pyramids of Giza in Egypt, the Christ the Redeemer statue in Rio de Janeiro, and the London Eye all turn green for St. Patrick's Day.

As we mentioned earlier, Halloween is another traditional Irish holiday that has spread around the world. People disguise themselves as spirits to protect themselves. People also carve turnips in Ireland for Samhain instead of pumpkins.

It's amazing how the traditions and folklore of the Irish are still burning brightly all around the world. Once you read more about the traditional mythology of Ireland, you will begin to recognize familiar names, places, and character references all throughout popular culture.

Chapter 2: The Creation Myths

Irish creation myths begin not with the creation of the entire world but with the beginning of Ireland.

There isn't just one single creation myth for the Irish people. In a Christian-related creation story, Cessair, a granddaughter of Noah, escaped the Great Flood with a small group of people. Unfortunately, there's a divine intervention, and everyone in their party dies aside from three people. Other creation myths (the most well known are the ones related to Partholón and Nemed) tell the story of waves of settlers who came to Ireland and faced various disasters and calamities.

In the story of Daghda and the Mórrígan, Daghda had a union with the Mórrígan, the goddess of death, on the eve of Samhain. The Mórrígan was a goddess who presided over battles, waiting to see death. She was a seductive shapeshifter, sometimes taking the form of a crow. The Celts understood that life and death walked closely alongside each other. The union of Daghda and the Mórrígan symbolized life, death, and rebirth.

Central to many Irish creation myths are the Tuatha Dé Danann, who arrived on the clouds bringing advanced knowledge and magic abilities. Their conflicts with other people groups in Ireland shaped the Irish landscape.

The Goddess Danu

Danu was the mother of the Tuatha Dé Danann, which is Gaelic for "people of the goddess Danu," pronounced *Thoo-a day Du-non*. Danu and her tribe of gods were skilled in craftsmanship, magic, music, and poetry. Danu is well known as a mother goddess and the most ancient of the Celtic gods. She's associated with rivers and farms, making her a goddess of fertility and abundance.

Very few stories of Danu remain. She appears in one important story with Bile, the god of light and healing. Bile was a sacred oak tree whom Danu fed and nurtured. Their union gave birth to Daghda, the equivalent of the Greek god Zeuss in importance.

Danu is also associated with the goddess Brigid. Some think they are one and the same. She was a powerful earth goddess, teacher, and warrior, making her an ancient Irish triple goddess.

The Battles of the Gods

The Battles of Moytura, otherwise known as Cath Maighe Tuireadh, are a set of two important battles in Irish mythology.

In the first battle, the Tuatha Dé Danann fought the current inhabitants of Ireland, the Fir Bolg.

Moytura are the Irish plains where the Tuatha Dé Danann first met the Fir Bolg. The Fir Bolg, along with their king Eochaid, resisted the arrival of the Tuatha Dé Danann into Ireland.

The epic battle began with a face-off between Sreng, the champion of Fir Bolg, and the Tuatha Dé Danann's King Nuada in one-on-one combat. Although King Nuada lost his arm during the battle, the Tuatha Dé Danann were the victors.

A Celtic king was required to be physically perfect. King Nuada couldn't rule the Tuatha Dé Danann while missing an arm. Nuada stepped down from leadership, and Bres, half Fomorian and half Tuatha Dé Danann, took his place. Quite unfortunately, Bres turned out to be a leader no one liked, as he was too oppressive.

Next, something mysterious and miraculous happened. The physician Dian Cécht of the Tuatha Dé Danann crafted a bionic silver arm that restored Nuada to physical perfection. (Keep in mind these were ancient times, long before any sort of surgery or medical advances.) Where did the Irish get this idea for their battle myth? No one is really sure. The silver arm was said to have the "vigor of every hand in it," meaning it had a full range of motion!

Nuada was a deity who knew pain and loss. He overcame his struggles to lead his people with courage and honor. He's considered a noble hero in Irish mythology.

As a final hurrah, the Mórrígan appeared on the battlefield to deliver a prophecy to the Tuatha Dé Danann. She predicted a second battle, during which blood would be shed.

The second battle took place on the sacred plains of Mag Tuired between the Tuatha Dé Danann and the Fomorians, who were otherworldly beings. This battle was more cosmic and symbolic than the first physical battle with the Fir Bolg. The Tuatha Dé Danann had become established as the ruling group when they were challenged by the Fomorians.

The central figure in this second battle was Lugh, a deity with many talents. Lugh was a master in battle, a craftsman, and talented at magic. In this battle, Lugh represented the importance of individuals with many abilities.

The Fomorians were led by their monstrous and terrifying king Balor, who had a destructive eye that could kill people with a mere glance, symbolizing wild chaos and destruction.

The myth of Lugh facing Balor in one-on-one combat symbolizes the battle between darkness and light. In this instance, light won out. Balor was killed when Lugh shot a stone with a slingshot and pierced Balor's powerful eye. This was a turning point in the battle, as light triumphed over darkness.

The Fomorians retreated, losing the battle. However, the war continued, as the Fomorians pledged to continue the battle from the depths of the sea.

The end of these two battles left the Tuatha Dé Danann as the victors over Ireland. The mythic qualities of these two stories remind us of the cyclical nature of life, the struggle between light and dark, and the battle between the divine and mortal realms.

The Giantess Cailleach

If you're from the United States, you'll be familiar with the yearly tradition of Groundhog's Day. Each year on February 2, as the folklore goes, the groundhog will emerge from hibernation. If he sees his shadow from the sun overhead, he will return to his burrow and winter will last six more weeks.

What does the groundhog's prediction have to do with Irish mythology? The tradition was brought to the United States by Germanic-speaking people (the Pennsylvania Dutch) and had roots in Celtic mythology. While we've lost the mythology from this tradition, we continue the tradition in the most basic form.

On February 1, as Celtic legend has it, the Giantess Cailleach, pronounced /kal-lay-ah/, ran out of firewood for the winter. In Irish tradition, she changes into her old woman form and goes out to collect firewood.

If the Cailleach wishes for winter to continue, she will make the day sunny. If the Cailleach sleeps in too late and doesn't start her search with a sunny morning, the day will be stormy and overcast.

If February 1 is sunny and pleasant, winter will return. If the day is overcast, winter will soon be over. This day is the holiday known as Imbolc, a traditional Gaelic festival that marks the halfway point between the winter solstice and the spring equinox. Officially, Imbolc marks the beginning of the spring season in Ireland. For Irish Catholics, Imbolc is also the feast day of St. Brigid (St. Brigid's Day), the patroness saint of Ireland.

Who is the Cailleach? She sounds considerably more mysterious than a simple groundhog, doesn't she? The Cailleach is considered one of the legendary ancestors of the Celts. She is both a creator deity and a divine old woman with extraordinary powers. We first see her featured in a poem from 900 CE, in which she is an old woman mourning the loss of her youth. She continued to appear in oral and written history through the twentieth century.

In Scottish and Irish Gaelic, the word *cailleach* simply means "old hag," or "old lady." The original word came from the similar old Gaelic term, *caillech*. In old Gaelic, it meant "veiled one" and was related to other words used for describing a woman.

The Cailleach has several forms, but her most common is that of an old woman, sometimes with only one eye. She always wears a veil. Through the veil, you can see her skin, which is blue tinged or very pale like a dead body. Her teeth have been described as rust red, and her clothing as adorned with skulls. She is powerful, possessing the ability to shapeshift into a large bird, leap across mountains, and ride on the air in ferocious storms. Her most powerful asset is her hammer, which can control thunder and the power of storms. She can also control a mysterious well, which at times might overflow and flood the land.

Some say the Cailleach was the personification of winter; her veil represents the land as it's covered with frost and snow. The Cailleach is also known as Cailleach Bhéara, which means she is the master of the winter months. On Samhain (October 31), the winter months begin, and the Cailleach returns to power. As we just learned, on February 2, the Cailleach collects her firewood and determines how much longer winter will last. As the sun grows stronger and summer approaches, the Cailleach weakens. On May 1 when the fertility festival Beltane is celebrated, the Cailleach transforms into Brigid, according to the lore in some areas.

In other stories, the Cailleach transfers her power to Brigid. In a last ditch effort to stop Brigid from taking power, the Cailleach brings turbulent storms to the land, but the warmth of the summer sun always wins out over the gray, cold winter wind.

She was both feared and respected by the Irish people. They knew she held their fate in her hands with the power of life or death as they struggled to get through the harshest months of the year.

Is the Cailleach good or evil?

While she appears as an intimidating dark force of nature, the Cailleach is not all bad. She is known for her tender and compassionate care of animals through the long winter months. The Cailleach is the patron of wolves. "Goddess of Grain" was another important role of the Cailleach. The last sheath of grain from the harvest was saved for her and used the next year to begin the spring planting.

Some say the Cailleach was the personification of female power and authority over a kingdom.

One story tells how the Cailleach meets the soon-to-be king. She looks like an ugly hag, but she invites him to have sexual relations with her. The king is repulsed, his reaction perhaps a metaphor for his feelings about kingship and becoming an adult. Eventually he gives in to the old hag, and after they make love, she is transformed into a beautiful young girl.

The age of the Cailleach is unknown. In Irish mythology, she's said to have seven maidenhoods, with numerous husbands, children, and foster children. She outlived them all and is known as the maternal ancestor of every Irish tribe.

As the story has it, a wandering friar and his scribe happened upon the home of the Cailleach. The friar had heard stories about the Cailleach being very old. He asked her age, and she told him she didn't know, but every year she made soup from an ox. When she was done, she always threw the bones up into the attic. Maybe, she suggested, they could count the bones to figure out her age.

The scribe climbed into the attic and threw the bones down one by one. As the bones came down, the friar put a mark on his paper for each bone. Soon, the friar had run out of paper and the pile of bones was huge. The scribe called down from the attic that he hadn't even moved all the bones from one corner of the attic and that the Cailleach must be extremely old.

According to Irish legend, the Cailleach was turned to stone.

The Cailleach Bhéara, or the Hag of Beara, has strong geographical ties to regions of Ireland. Because of her ability to form landscapes and grow mountains by dropping or tossing stones from her cloak, she is often tied to coastal and mountain locations. She can be found at Hag's Head on the Cliffs of Moher, in County Clare, where the cliffs make an odd rock formation that resembles a woman's head looking out to sea.

Sliabh na Caillí, otherwise known as Hag's Mountain, in County Meath, is dotted with ancient cairns. When the Cailleach jumped from hill to hill, she dropped stones that formed the cairns. If you visit the area today, you can sit on the Hag's chair. If you make a wish while sitting on the chair, legend says the witch will make it come true.

The Cailleach's home is said to be Beara Peninsula. This place also claims to be her final grave. Cailleach Bhéara's fossilized body overlooks Coulagh Bay, Eyeries, as she waits for the return of her husband, the sea god Manannán mac Lir.

Chapter 3: The Tuatha Dé Danann

The Fir Bolg were ruling ancient Ireland, minding their own business, when one day there was a sudden stir in the air. Dark clouds and mist rushed overhead, filling the sky. Strange flying ships came into view, engulfed in the dark clouds, carrying the Tuatha Dé Danann into Ireland. The ships landed on a mountain in County Leitrim. The dark clouds that followed them were so thick they blocked out the sunlight for the following three days.

Out of the ships descended this mysterious race of magical beings. They were exceptionally tall and very pale, with red or blond hair and blue or green eyes. The Tuatha Dé Danann were gorgeous and magical. Their origins seemed shrouded in mystery.

We introduced the Tuatha Dé Danann in the first chapter of this book, but there is quite a bit more to be said about them, as they are one of the key players in the Mythological Cycle of Irish history.

Did this supernatural race of beings actually arrive in Ireland in flying ships, riding the waves of mist and fog? Some swear it's true. Over the centuries, people have gone as far as to speculate that the Tuatha Dé Danann were aliens. Other legends say they came on regular ships in the ocean, explaining that the fog and dark clouds were caused by their ships burning after their arrival on land.

But wait! Where did the Tuatha Dé Danann originate from? They didn't just appear out of the mist. Their true origins have been as hotly debated as their methods of travel.

Folklore tells us they were a supernatural race residing in what the Irish called the "Otherworld." It is also known as, or contains, Tír na nÓg (pronounced teer na noog), a place where everyone had everlasting youth, pleasure, knowledge, and peace. They were able to interact with everyone living in the "real world."

Tír na nÓg has four magical cities: Falias, Gorias, Findias, and Murias.

Tír na nÓg is always described vividly in Irish mythology. The meadows are the lushest of green grasses. The lakes sparkle like clear crystal. The forests are illuminated with a shimmering glow that is beautiful beyond what humans experience on Earth. Overhead, birds sing sweet melodies.

Everyone in Tír na nÓg is immortal, even the birds. Time passes differently there than on Earth. Tír na nÓg isn't a place where people go after death; instead, it's an earth-like place. It is one of the Otherworld places that gods and goddesses travel to once they are finished being deities.

Tír na nÓg is located just beyond the western edge of the world. Mortals living in Ireland can visit Tír na nÓg by invitation or by undertaking an arduous journey across the seas. Tír na nÓg can only be reached by magic. Sometimes visitors enter through cairns in ancient burial grounds. This beautiful Otherworld is ruled by Manannán mac Lir, a member of the Tuatha Dé Danann who is said to be the God of the Dead, the God of the Sea, and the first ancestor of the human race.

Visits paid by mortals to Tír na nÓg inspired many stories in Irish mythology and folklore. These stories are called echtrai, which translates to "adventures," or baili, which means "visions."

Often, mortal heroes are drawn to Tír na nÓg by the beautiful goddesses. This symbolizes the power the Celts gave to women. In the ancient Celtic worldview, the essence of the creative universe was female. Many times the hero had to complete tasks and would then return to the mortal world, bringing with him a higher state of being.

While it's a magical Otherworld of happiness, Tír na nÓg can also be a dangerous place for humans. Legends say the greatest danger is for those who stay for periods of three, like three days, three months, or three years.

Oisín and Niamh

Perhaps the most famous tale of Tír na nÓg is that of Oisín and Niamh (pronounced Neeve).

Niamh, which means "bright" or "radiant," is a stunning goddess of the Tuatha Dé Danann with golden hair. Her father was Manannán mac Lir, and she was a queen of the Tír na nÓg Otherworld.

Niamh fell hard in love with Oisín, the son of Finn (pronounced as oh-Sheen), who was chief of the infamous Fenian Celtic warriors of ancient Ireland.

Niamh had a beautiful white horse named Embarr, meaning "imagination."

Embarr could run and jump over the waves of the sea, running across the surface at a fast speed. Symbolically, Embarr ran across the surface of the sea while life, death, and regeneration existed silently, running in the depths below her. Embarr represented freedom, endurance, and spirit. Niamh used the power of intention, or imagination, to fly across the seas from Tír na nÓg to Ireland. Wild, crashing white waves often look like white horses running across the water, reminding the Irish people of Niamh every time they gaze out at the white-capped Atlantic Ocean.

As Niamh arrived among the Fenian warriors, she discovered Oisín, who was both a warrior and poet. He couldn't resist her shining beauty, and he excitedly accepted the invitation to ride Embarr alongside her. He was willingly transported back across the sea to the Otherworld of eternal youth, Tír na nÓg.

After arriving in Tír na nÓg, Oisín spent what seemed to him like three blissful years with Niamh. Tír na nÓg was a land of singularity—only joy and happiness existed there, no illness or fear. Oisín loved Tír na nÓg, but he began to long for his home back in Ireland, the land of duality where he had both joy and struggle. In Oisín's mind, he only wanted to visit his home, not leave Tír na nÓg permanently and give up the land of singular bliss.

Niamh understood his longing, though she didn't want to let her love go. She loaned Embarr to Oisín, giving him the ability to journey back to Ireland. There was only one caveat. Niamh warned Oisín that his feet must not touch the soil of Ireland. He had to stay on Embarr. If his feet touched land, his life on Earth would claim him, and he would be barred from returning to Tír na nÓg forever.

With this warning in his mind, Oisín began his journey to Ireland. What Oisín didn't fully understand was the amount of change his soul had experienced while living in the land of light and love. He had moved to a higher state of being, and his soul couldn't go back to its previous fully human state of existence.

When he arrived in Ireland, he was shocked to learn that far more than three years had passed. In fact, it had actually been three hundred years. His friends and family were gone. His normal reality was gone forever. He remained astride Embarr, turning her around to head back to Niamh in Tír na nÓg. Just before reaching the sea to begin his return journey, he came across a group of people who were trying to move a large rock blocking the roadway.

Oisín knew he couldn't dismount from his horse and touch the soil, so he bent over from the saddle to help move the rock out of the way. This was when the unthinkable happened to Oisín. The saddle strap broke. He fell from the saddle and landed on Irish soil. The moment his feet touched Irish soil, he lost Niamh's protection. In the blink of an eye, Embarr disappeared. Oisín was transformed from a strong, vibrant man into an old person. From that moment, he was barred from returning to the land of youth and forever separated from his love Niamh on the human plane.

The men on the road were horrified as they witnessed Oisín changing into an old man quickly before their eyes. They rushed him to St. Patrick, who tried to comfort the man. When Oisín learned that his father and their people, the Fianna, were completely gone from Ireland, he was filled with despair.

He told St. Patrick many stories about his father and how they fought and hunted together. He then told St. Patrick all about his beautiful golden-haired wife, Niamh, the love of his life, and the years he had spent in Tír na nÓg.

Oisín died a few days later since he was very old and weak. The stories he shared have lived on forever in Irish legends, becoming the basis for Tír na nÓg in Irish mythology and folktales.

Back in Tír na nÓg, Niamh waited for Oisín. She knew deep within that Oisín had returned to the land of duality, to Ireland. Shortly after Oisín departed Tír na nÓg, Niamh gave birth to his child, a daughter she named Plur na mBan, the "flower of women." Plur na mBan became the fairy queen of Beltane, the Celtic holiday celebrated on May 1, representing life and renewal.

Plur na mBan completed Niamh and Oisín's family, joining their two sons, Finn and Oscar.

Eventually, pining for her love Oisín, Niamh journeyed to earth in search of him. She found the answer she had known deep within her heart. Oisín had been transformed into an old man and died, gone forever from Earth, never again to be reunited with Niamh.

In a way, the story of Niamh and Oisín is a reverse Adam and Eve story. Niamh did not tempt Oisín at all, simply inviting him to join her in Tír na nÓg. The two lovebirds left the land of struggle and joys for the land of eternal peace and happiness.

Mag Tuired

As Earth was a place of duality, the Tuatha Dé Danann experienced both joy and struggle while existing on the human plane. Part of that struggle included war, which they carried out bravely on the plain of Mag Tuired. You may remember the description of the Tuatha Dé Danann's two famous battles from the previous chapter, the Battle of the Gods.

The Fomorians, the Tuatha Dé Danann's opponents in the second battle, were giants, evil monstrous beings who came from under the earth or the sea. Their battle with the Tuatha Dé Danann is portrayed as a war between the gods. Their defeat allowed present-day Irish culture to spread across the island through the Tuatha Dé Danann.

Despite being enemies, the Tuatha Dé Danann sometimes intermarried with the Fomorians. Historians have pointed out that the Viking raids on Ireland took place around the same time as this war between the Tuatha Dé Danann and the Fomorians.

The Defeat of the Tuatha Dé Danann

After defeating the Fomorians, peace reigned over the area for more than a hundred years until, one day, the Milesians arrived. Thought to be an Iberian Spanish people group, the Milesians are believed to have come to Ireland to avenge the death of one of their famous wizards that had been recently killed by the Tuatha Dé Danann. The Milesians were the first Gaels to inhabit Ireland.

As legend goes, the Tuatha Dé Danann asked the Milesians to anchor their ships nine waves away from shore for three days for a truce. The Milesians agreed, but the Tuatha Dé Danann created a fierce magical storm in an attempt to get rid of the Milesians.

The Milesians had a magical poet in their midst named Amergin, who calmed the seas with his verse. His well-known chant says,

"I am the wind which blows over the sea,

I am the wave of the ocean,

I am the bull of seven battles,

I am the eagle on the rock . . .

I am a boar for courage,

I am a salmon in the water . . ."

The calming of the storm allowed the Milesians to land ashore. The Milesians then defeated the Tuatha Dé Danann at a place called Tailtiu, present-day Teltown in County Meath.

After the Milesians' victory, the poet Amergin was asked to divide Ireland between the two races. The poet was clever. He outsmarted the Tuatha Dé Danann and made their allotment of Ireland underground while giving the entirety of the above-ground land to the Milesians.

What happened next?

This was an important historical turning point for Irish mythology. It was here that the Tuatha Dé Danann were led underground by their leader, Manannán mac Lir, passing through the sidhe (burial mounds). Each one of the Tuatha Dé Danann tribes was given their own mound. There, they entered an underground plane of existence that was part of the Tír na nÓg Otherworld noted to be filled with flowers and honey. This story is told in *Immram Brain*, The Voyage of Bran.

Entrance to tunnel at Newgrange.
Internet Archive Book Images, No restrictions, via Wikimedia Commons;
https://commons.wikimedia.org/wiki/File:Myths_and_legends;_the_Celtic_race_(1910)_(14596737390).jpg

That is what became of the Tuatha Dé Danann.

From this point on, the existed parallel to the human world, showing up endlessly in Irish folklore. They are considered by some to be the same as fairies. They are stunningly gorgeous and can be good and kind, but at other times, they can be nasty and vicious.

Symbolism and Influence in Present-day Irish Culture

Let's pause for a side note before we continue discussing the history and reputation of the sidhe in Irish folklore.

You may have noticed that the symbolism of threes is prevalent throughout both Celtic and Irish myths. In the love story of Niamh and Oisín, remember how Oisín thought he stayed in the Otherworld for three years, but it was actually three hundred years? And, when the Tuatha Dé Danann first arrived in Ireland, they made the sky dark with clouds for three days. Symbols of three can be found everywhere in Irish storytelling, if you keep an eye out for them.

The main symbolism behind the number three in the stories is the idea of life, death, and rebirth. The Celts believed that the human soul was indestructible, simply passing from one form to another. Three also represented the Celtic belief that the world was made up of earth, water, and sky. The family unit was also marked by threes with the father, mother, and child.

Some of you may be thinking of the Holy Trinity and the importance of three in Christianity, but remember, the earliest Irish mythology predates Christianity and the arrival of Christian monks to the isle. Later in Irish folklore, three can also represent the three worlds: Earth, Heaven, and Purgatory, showing the influence of Christianity.

The ultimate representation of three is the Triskele. This simple symbol shows three spirals fused together. It goes back as far as Neolithic times, linking ancient Celtic civilizations, including the Irish.

Triskele pattern.

For thousands of years, the Triskele symbol was carved into various objects, on monuments, and in art all across Celtic cultures, especially in the areas of Ireland, Wales, Scotland, and Britany.

Overall, the spiral is meant to represent the concept of life, death, and rebirth. The three spirals joined together add the additional significance of infinity. Each spiral represents a different element in the never-ending cycle. The first spiral represents the mother, who embodies creation and birth. The second spiral is for the father, who symbolizes life and existence. The third spiral is for the child, who gives new beginnings and the promise of a future.

The spirals show the conductive flow of energy as they weave together, uniting the physical and spiritual planes. Today, the three interwoven spirals also represent the continual link the Irish people have between their past, present, and future through their cultural heritage.

Chapter 4: The Sidhe

Every civilization around the world believes in some sort of unseen world populated by spirits. These spirits are surrounded by myths and legends we try to understand through the lens of our own limited human viewpoint and experiences.

Christianity believes in angels, Catholic saints, demons, and the souls of humans after death. For the Irish, there are the ancient gods and goddesses, the people of the Celtic Otherworld, and the sidhe, or the fairies.

The land of Ireland, with its countryside of rolling hills, shadows, and glimmering patches of light, cliffs, large rocks, and crashing waves, lends itself to legend and folklore. It provides the perfect backdrop for human interaction with the gods and goddesses and the partially obscured world of the fairies. In fact, the inhabitants of Ireland have always had a deep spiritual connection with the land.

The first mention of "noble" fairies were beings that appeared tall and human-like. These were the Tuatha Dé Danann discussed in previous chapters. Here is a brief recap of where we left off with their story:

When the Milesians witnessed the beauty and magical talents of the Tuatha Dé Danann, they decided not to defeat them and destroy this unique group of beings. According to some versions of the legend, especially in the De Gabáil in t-Sída ("The Taking of the Sí"), they instead tricked the Tuatha Dé Danann into going below ground to rule, leaving the above-ground world to the Milesian people. Others say the Tuatha Dé Danann split the rule of the land into Above and Below with the Milesians willingly. Either way, the Tuatha Dé Danann are said to have gone below the land through the sidhe, the burial mounds dotting the landscape of Ireland.

From here, in hidden places all over the isle, they built forts and palaces. They held high parties, filled with singing and chanting, and mourned being exiled from Ireland above.

The Tuatha Dé Danann became known as the sidhe, named after the burial mounds they used as portals to their realm. (In Gaelic, *aos sí*, or *sidhe*, means "people of the mounds.") Their realm is called Land of the Fairy (Fairyland), an Otherworld. In Gaelic, the Otherworlds are called *An Saol Eile*.

Are all of the fairies descended from the Tuatha Dé Danann? The answer to that seems to be no, though a multitude of legends and folklore sometimes contradict. Tales and stories were passed by word of mouth rather than written down for hundreds of years, meaning variations changed based on locations. Many things about the sidhe remain cloaked in mystery, and that's part of the charm and magic of the fairy realm.

Believers in the sidhe say there are different races or tribes of fairy folk. They can affect what happens in the human realm, though they often do so secretly so that the humans aren't aware of their interference until after the fact.

The sidhe travel over the land of Ireland through the mountains and hills. They can be found in lakes, bogs, and caves all over the islands. They usually remain invisible to the human eye. When they appear, they will usually be human-like in nature. Some, like the leprechaun, are small in stature, but for the most part, they are average-sized and often exceptionally beautiful.

While the name sidhe is connected to the ancient burial mounds, it also has a meaning in the modern Irish language, Gaeilge (Irish Gaelic). The term *sí* represents either the mounds or the fairy being.

There are several terms that include sí:

- *Bean sí* means "fairy woman, banshee"
- *An slua sí* means "the fairy host"
- *Long sí* means "phantom ship"
- *Ceol sí* means "enchanting music"
- *Solas sí* means "misguiding light"
- *Sí gaoithe* means "whirlwind, fairy wind"

Irish tradition says it may be unlucky or anger the fairies with your disrespect if you refer to them directly by the term "fairy." Other terms like "fae" or "faeries" aren't used in Ireland. In fact, some people will go to desperate lengths with long, twisting descriptions to avoid referring to the sidhe by name.

Want to know some of the popular alternate descriptions to talk about fairies without actually saying their name?

Some other names for the sidhe include:

- *Aes sídhe, aos sí,* or *daoine sidhe,* meaning "people, or folk, of the mounds"
- *Na daoine uaisle,* meaning "the noble people"
- *Na uaisle,* which indicates noble or highborn status
- *Na daoine maithe,* meaning "the good people"
- *An slua sí, slúagh sídhe,* meaning "the fairy host or crowd"
- The fair folk
- Themselves
- The other crowd
- The people of the hills
- The gentry

Types of Irish Fairies

Irish legends and myths don't differentiate between groups of fairies as good or bad. Much of the fairy realm aligns with a particular location or Irish province. Legend has it that you may meet a fairy if you follow a fairy path. Fairies won't be evil spirits in most cases, but they are also not like the tiny, woodland fairies made up by pop culture and Western media.

Here are a few types of Irish fairies you could encounter:

The Banshee or Bean Sidhe

"'Twas the banshee's lonely wailing

Well I knew the voice of death,

On the night wind slowly sailing,

O'er the bleak and gloomy heath.

By 'O' or 'Mac', you'll always know

True Irishmen they say,

But if they lack an 'O' or 'Mac'

No Irishmen are they!"

- Fairy Legends and Traditions of the South of Ireland by T. C. Croker

Perhaps the most misunderstood of the fairies is the banshee.

Pop culture has created a banshee that belongs in a horror movie, a demonic creature that screams to incite terror. In reality, this is far from the truth. The bean sidhe, or banshee, as we now spell it in English (pronounced "ban shee"), is actually a mournful woman who is believed to be attached to the lineage of certain Irish families. She will appear before a death, keening and wailing to mourn her distant family member's passing. She is there to guide souls to their next destination or ensure people who have done terrible things in this life remain chained to the mortal plane to suffer their penance.

Most of the time the banshee will wail alone, but when someone important is going to die, banshees will appear together. It is a rare occurrence to see banshees keen in a chorus for someone holy or great. When this happens, the banshees will travel in a carriage known as the *cóiste bodhar* (pronounced "coach-a-bower"), a large black coach with a coffin on it. Pulling the coffin are headless horses. The coach is driven by Dullahan.

This part of banshee mythology turns away from the mournful woman and goes toward a darker, more frightening place. The Dullahan is the embodiment of the Celtic god Crom Dubh. Unlike the banshee, he does take souls. He is the headless horseman who roams the night searching for souls to steal.

Some stories say he is angry and bitter about losing his own head in battle as a soldier. Now he roams the countryside looking for other souls to take. Other folklore says he is just mourning his life and searching for his own head.

A popular quote chanted by children goes,

> "If you ever hear the banshee cry,
>
> Someone you love is soon to die.
>
> Three days after her frightful song,
>
> Your beloved companion will soon be gone."

We will discuss many details and stories related to the banshee in a later chapter of this book.

For now, I will leave you to muse over this banshee folktale, first published by Jane Wilde in her book *Ancient Legends, Mystic Charms &*

There was once a gentleman who had a lovely daughter. She was a beautiful girl, the perfect picture of health. She was a horsewoman, and she enjoyed riding behind the hounds during every hunt. The men admired both her beauty and her riding skill.

One evening after the hunt was completed, there was a ball. The girl danced and danced, while everyone whispered that she possessed the grace of a fairy queen.

That same night, as her father was sleeping, a voice came very close to his bedroom window, so close in fact that it seemed as if the person speaking was pressed up against the glass. The father heard a mourning wail, almost a song.

Then, as a chill passed through his body, he heard the words ringing out into the night air, "In three weeks death; in three weeks the grave-dead-dead-dead!"

He heard the voice crying out those words three times over. He jumped out of bed and looked out into the bright moonlight, but he didn't see anyone there.

To his complete horror, the next morning, his daughter awoke with a fever. After three weeks of illness, the bean sidhe's prophecy came true. His lovely daughter was dead.

The night before his daughter passed away, everyone heard very soft music outside of the house. The family peered out of the windows and saw the form of an old woman crouching beneath the trees. She had a cloak covering her head.

They walked outside to see who this woman was, but as they got closer, she disappeared into the mist. Her music continued playing softly until the day dawned. The daughter then died.

The prophecy of the bean sidhe had come true, just as the mysterious spirit voice at the father's window had said.

Cat Sí (Fairy Cat) and Cú Sí (Fairy Hound)

There is some debate whether the cat sí is a true fairy or a witch. One popular folk tale says that cat sí is a witch who can change into a cat nine times. On the ninth time, she will be stuck as a cat forevermore. This is likely the source behind the common phrase, "Cats have nine lives."

If you see a cat sí, it will appear much larger than a regular domesticated house cat. It will be similar to the size of a large dog, with a very long shaggy tail that could be curly. The coloring of the cat sí is always dark, ranging from dark green to black in hue. At times, the cat sí is noted to appear as a white cat with red ears, which is a common fairy animal coloring across all Celtic myths, not just in Ireland. Other stories, especially those of the Scottish Highlands, say the cat sí (or cat síth) is a black cat with a white spot on its chest, similar to the tuxedo cats common in the US today.

Cú sí, or cú sídhe, is the canine counterpart to the fairy cat. This hound lives in the clefts of craggy rocks, especially in the Scottish Highlands, though he has also been known to make an appearance in Irish mythology. His coat is shaggy and dark green, and he is the size of a small cow. The cú sídhe is said to hunt silently through the rocks until he lets out three absolutely terrifying barks that are so loud they can carry for miles, all the way across the land to the sea. Legend has it that if you do not find safety by his third bark, you will perish from pure terror.

Changeling

The changeling is a common story character in many, many stories told by the average person in Ireland for hundreds of years. These stories are frightening, especially because they often involve the fairies switching out babies with a changeling, while the real baby is carried off to the fairy Otherworld. The fairies place an enchantment on an ugly creature or a piece of wood, making it appear lovely and very much the same as the stolen child, though the child may be badly behaved or stop growing normally. Some folklore says they could begin to grow pointed teeth or even a beard. The enchantment tricks the mother and father into thinking nothing's wrong at first.

At some point, the fairies usually reveal themselves, likely by accident, by doing or saying something a baby would not be able to do. This is usually speaking, singing, dancing, or saying something wise beyond their years. In other cases, someone wiser than the parents will visit the family and see the enchanted changeling, then realize what has happened. This could be a wise woman, a fairy doctor, or simply a nosy neighbor.

At this point, the family would test the changeling to see what it truly was. Unfortunately, these tests were often dangerous for a normal child, who may have caused suspicion just by acting abnormally or becoming ill. Sometimes, the tests would include exposing the child to fire or leaving them out in the elements, causing actual harm to an innocent baby.

The nineteenth and twentieth centuries have many tragic family tales where children and young adults were accused of being changelings and harmed by mistake.

At times, the fairies would steal adult humans. Newlywed women and new mothers were a favorite of the fairies. Young people were snatched away and sent to the Otherworld to marry fairies instead of their human spouse. If an adult was captured by the fairies, a log or something similar would be left behind, enchanted to appear like the missing person. The enchanted object would slowly get sick and die, making the family think they were mourning and burying their loved one. All the while, the real human was living among the fairies.

The Story of Bridget Cleary

Similar to the stories of children being harmed, there were also cases where adults were hurt when they were accused of being changelings. The story of Bridget Cleary is very well known in Ireland.

Bridget Cleary was born as Bridget Boland on February 19, 1869. She was from Ballyvadlea in County Tipperary, Ireland. Her childhood was unremarkable; she was an average young woman who worked as a dressmaker's apprentice. On August 6, 1887, she married Michael Cleary in a Roman Catholic church in Drangan. She had only known him for a month. They were married for eight years when Michael noticed a change in his wife. He believed she had been taken by the fairies and that she had become a changeling.

Despite being married eight years, the couple had no children together. After getting married, Bridget had decided to go home to be with her parents in Ballyvadlea. Michael stayed in Clonmel, working as a cooper. Bridget flourished while they lived apart. She raised chickens and sold their eggs for money. She used the money to purchase a sewing machine, and she worked hard as a dressmaker and a milliner. At one point, her mother died, leaving Bridget to care for her elderly father. Bridget and Michael were not laborers, but her father Patrick had been one in his youth. This qualified them to live in a laborer's house with the elderly Patrick.

The nicest house in the village was a laborer's house, but it stood empty. No one wanted to live there because it was rumored to be built on a fairy ringfort.

In March 1895, Bridget became ill. The doctor had diagnosed her with bronchitis on March 13, but she was so ill that a priest was called to the house to give her the last rites within a few days. Her friends and family visited, carrying out the traditions needed for the final days of someone's life. However, Bridget's father and husband grew angry, accusing her of being a fairy changeling and not simply the very ill Bridget. They threw urine on the poor sick woman, then drug her over to the fireplace in an attempt to cast out the fairy. Her husband wanted to force the fairies to return his true bride.

On March 19, Bridget's friends and family heard rumors she was missing. This was reported to the police, who began the search for her. Michael was heard saying that his wife had been taken by the fairies, and he held a vigil for her return.

The police began to gather statements from witnesses. Eventually, on March 22, her burned body was found in a shallow grave. Nine people were charged with her disappearance and death, her husband included. The coroner determined Bridget had died by being burned to death. After the discovery of Bridget's body, there was a court case. Her husband and the eight others were convicted. Her husband was charged with manslaughter and spent fifteen years in prison.

Leprechauns

A leprechaun working on a shoe.
https://commons.wikimedia.org/wiki/File:Goble-Book_of_Fairy_Poetry024Lupracaun_or_Fairy_Shoemaker.jpg)

"Up the airy mountain,
Down the rushy glen,
We daren't go a-hunting
For fear of little men."

-"The Fairies," William Allingham

Finally, we have arrived at perhaps the most popular fairy in the Western world: the leprechaun!

In the United States, the mischievous leprechaun is the key cartoon character on a popular children's cereal. He is connected with the holiday St. Patrick's Day, and every child knows that he leaves a pot of gold at the end of the rainbow.

Perhaps lesser known, but still part of modern-day culture, is the leprechaun's ability to make and mend shoes. He can also mysteriously refill a purse or a pot with coins, like the hallmark bucket of gold. He can also turn himself invisible, aiding in his mischief.

Before the nineteenth century, there wasn't an established leprechaun across Ireland like there is today. There were regional variations, including the cluricaune of County Cork, the luricaune of Kerry, the lurigadaune of Tipperary, the leprechaun of Leinster, and the loghery man of Ulster.

The different variations of the leprechaun came to be as the oral tradition was shared across different regions and each storyteller added a bit of their own flare. Sometimes, one part of the story was misunderstood, and the tale was changed to a new version as it was repeated between families and friends.

The name "cluricaune" came from the term *cliobar ceann*, which means "merry head," representing this fairy's love for the drink. As the folklore went, the leprechaun came from *leath brogan*, which means "half of a shoe." This is where we got the idea that he is a shoemaker, which bears a similarity to the elves from Grimm's Fairy Tales.

When the leprechauns first appeared in stories that had been written down, they were called *luchorpán,* which means "little body." The folklore claimed that luchorpáns were descendants of Noah's son Ham in the Bible, who was cursed. The Fomorian giants and other monsters were also said to be descendants of Ham. It's interesting that the wee green men fell into the same category. Some scholars today think that this claim could have been a misunderstanding. They believe the name could instead be something from the time of the Romans.

In almost every story, the leprechaun had one assignment. He was sent to guard treasure. The legends say anyone who outsmarts him can take the treasure for themselves. This story likely came about because the Irish people love a good story involving gold coins and hidden treasure. History left Ireland full of possible gold coins and treasures that were hidden by invaders over the years. The Vikings, for example, hid gold in the monasteries.

The leprechaun carries a small purse that will never run out of gold coins. Legend has it that if you manage to capture a leprechaun, you can take as many coins as you want from his purse because you will never reach the bottom. The key is not letting the leprechaun escape from you!

The leprechaun is very clever. He is always ready to trick you. He might switch his bottomless purse for a regular one. He might become invisible and vanish the moment you take your eyes off him.

Tim O'Donovan

One story tells of a man named Tim O'Donovan. He lived in Kerry. Tim captured a leprechaun way out in the bog on his property and forced the leprechaun to reveal the location of the treasure he was guarding. The leprechaun revealed the location, and Tim realized he needed to mark the spot so he could come back later with a spade to dig it up.

Looking around, Tim found a stick to put in the ground, marking the spot where the leprechaun had pointed. He rested his hat on top of the stick just for good measure, fully planning to come back and dig the next day.

The following morning, a very excited Tim O'Donovan marched himself right back into the bog, spade in hand, ready to dig up his riches. To his dismay, he got a terrible surprise. Everywhere he looked, as far as he could see, there were hundreds of identical sticks shoved into the ground. Each one had a hat identical to his own resting on top.

He examined many sticks and hats carefully, but he couldn't tell any difference between them. There was no way of knowing which was the original hat and stick. After some time, he walked out of the bog empty-handed with his head hanging low, cursing the leprechaun for tricking him. The leprechaun was nowhere to be seen, having disappeared into the mist hours ago.

There are stories of the leprechaun, or the luchorpán, written in the Mythological and Ulster Cycles' stories that give us a far more in-depth character study of the simple leprechaun tricksters we know from popular folklore.

The Ulster Porridge Pot

The first story, which tells of King Lubdan, King Fergus, and the infamous Ulster Porridge Pot, is one example of a tale with great insight into the leprechaun world. The story was first put to paper in 1517, but the original tale is estimated to have originated around the eighth century.

The story tells of two very different Irish societies that fear each other. The two groups come together and gain an understanding of one another. The unique aspect of this story is that it comes from the point of view of the fairies. The leprechauns tell their side of events, revealing how complex their society is.

The story opens with King Fergus mac Léti of Ulster. The king called for a feast to take place at his fort. It just so happened that, at that very time, another king was also planning a wonderful feast in another fort, in a different realm. This second king was King Lubdan, the king of the leprechauns, otherwise known as the Wee Folk. His land was called Faylinn.

King Lubdan called together all his lords, his princes, and his heir, who was named Beag, son of Beg. Queen Bebo was also at the banquet, along with the strongman Glower, who was famous for being the strongest in Faylinn. Glower's most famous strongman feat was the ability to knock down a thistle with a single swing of his ax.

The guests at the leprechaun King Lubdan's banquet enjoyed large, juicy rabbit legs, the ribs of field mice, and plenty of wine. The king was overcome with love for his people and his kingdom. Perhaps he was also a little bit drunk on wine, who knows.

The king stood up at the table and yelled out, "Has anyone ever seen a king who is more wonderful and amazing than I am? Or a king that possesses more power than me?"

The wee leprechaun folk all yelled back, "No, never!"

"Have you ever seen any warriors or cavalry that could beat the men at this feast?"

"Never!" the wee folk screamed back at their king.

"What about a stronger man than our giant Glower?" asked King Lubdan.

"We swear we have never!" they responded back.

Lubdan felt very self-assured, and he told them, "I promise you, anyone who tries to conquer our kingdom would struggle. We are so strong and fierce!"

It was then that, amidst the cheering, laughter broke out from the corner of the room. The king's chief poet Eisirt was laughing so hard he lost his breath. The king was incensed with rage and demanded that Eisirt explain his laughter. Eisirt apologized, and it was then he explained something shocking to the leprechauns.

"I know of another place in Ireland where just a single man could take down the Kingdom of Faylinn and fit all the people at this table in one single porridge pot, without even filling the pot all the way full!"

The king demanded Eisirt be arrested at once for his disrespect. As he was being taken away, Eisirt called out a prophecy. He said horrible events would come to the king because of his arrest. Eisirt told the king he would go himself to the human realm in Ireland and find proof of the giant race to show the king he wasn't lying. The king was curious at this point. He agreed to let Eisirt free, so Eisirt began his quest.

After some time, Eisirt reached Emhain Mhacha, where King Fergus lived. The king's guards were shocked when they looked down and saw a miniscule nobleman. Eisirt was wearing beautiful silk sewn into a tunic. His cloak was bright red. He carried a poet's rod, which was made of gleaming white bronze metal. The rod was so tiny it looked to be the size of a needle to King Fergus' guards. The gatekeeper rushed away to inform the king of this unique visitor to his kingdom.

King Fergus didn't understand. He told the gatekeeper that he already had a little person in his court. He was referring to a human of small statue, not a fairy. Fergus asked if this visitor was smaller than his poet Aedh. Aedh was also a wise man, well versed in the sciences, and the chief poet for the kingdom.

The gatekeeper told him yes, this visitor was much smaller than Aedh. The gatekeeper told the king that the visitor was indeed so tiny that he could stand on Aedh's palm. The lords and ladies overheard this statement and immediately ran outside to see Eisirt at the gates. They were fascinated by his tiny size and his lovely clothing, so they carried him back inside to their hall, where the king was waiting.

King Fergus stared in amazement at the wee person. He demanded, "Who are you?"

Eisirt answered proudly, "I am Eisirt, the chief poet of the Kingdom of Faylinn, bard, and rhymer of the luchra and lupracan."

Eisirt was a very charming little fellow. He told the king, the lords, and the ladies all the enchanting tales of Faylinn. They offered him gifts, but he didn't accept any of them.

After staying three days and three nights with the king, he wanted to return home to Faylinn.

The poet Aedh asked if he could go with Eisirt back to the Kingdom of Faylinn. Aedh was a small human, so small that he could lie on a warrior and only take up space on their chest. Next to Eisirt, he was quite the giant, however. He desperately wanted to experience a land where everyone was far tinier than him.

To get to Faylinn, they had to journey over the waves, speeding through time and space on Eisirt's red-maned hare. Eisirt told Aedh that it was Lubdan's horse.

There were leprechauns waiting on the shore to spot Eisirt returning across the waves back to the Fairy realm and the Kingdom of Faylinn. When they spotted Aedh riding the red-maned hare, they were filled with both awe and terror. They were certain Aedh had come to kill them all, as he was surely a giant from the human realm. Eisirt laughed as he told them that Aedh was a poet and a wise man from the human realm, but he was also the smallest man in the human kingdom.

King Lubdan was slightly angry that Eisirt had been proven correct. The whole kingdom of Faylinn was actually tiny in comparison to the other kingdoms? He hadn't realized, and he didn't like this idea. He had it in his head that he would now have to travel to the land of these human giants to see for himself.

Eisirt gave a warrior's challenge to the king. He challenged him to go to Ulster and have a taste of the king's royal porridge, which was famous in the entire human realm. King Lubdan and Queen Bebo accepted Eisirt's challenge. They climbed their sleek hare once nightfall arrived and sped over the waves to the land of the humans. They arrived early in the morning, while the entire kingdom lay sleeping.

For some reason (shyness perhaps, or maybe Lubdan was just bold), they decided to sneak into the palace rather than greet the guards at the gate. Lubdan made his way straight to the kitchen to locate this famous pot of Ulster porridge.

To the little king's dismay, the pot was so tall that he couldn't get to the rim. He stood upon his hare and managed to get up to the top of the pot. As he reached forward, grasping for the silver ladle in the full pot of porridge, he slipped, tumbling in. The porridge inside the pot was cool but thick. It held him tight, like glue. He couldn't move a muscle!

King Lubdan began to panic. The humans would soon wake up for the morning, and what then? He decided to sing a sad song to Queen Bebo, who was waiting outside the pot, crying out to her for help. In his song, he told her she would be foolish to stay and be caught along with him.

Bebo refused to abandon the king. She promised him she would watch and wait to see what happened. When the humans came down to the kitchen a few minutes later, they were confused to see a very tiny man trapped in the pot of porridge, with a very tiny woman weeping sadly outside of the porridge pot.

The men began laughing, and they immediately rescued the sticky Lubdan from the pot and whisked him upstairs to see King Fergus.

King Fergus realized this wasn't the same leprechaun that had visited a few days prior. King Lubdan told him, "I am king of the luchra folk. This is my wife, Queen Bebo."

The king was nervous, having heard of fairy mischief, so he told them to take Lubdan to a room and watch him closely. Lubdan assured the king that he was an honest leprechaun. The king decided he could give Lubdan and Bebo a nice room within the palace, but he wouldn't allow them to leave. He asked them to share their wisdom and fairy knowledge with the lords and ladies in his court.

After some time, the leprechauns showed up at the palace to demand the return of their king. They brought seven battalions of wee folk and cried for King Lubdan to be given back to them.

King Fergus, not one to do anything out of the goodness of his heart, asked the leprechauns what ransom they would give for their king.

The leprechauns offered to cover the king's fields with corn every year, but the king scoffed at this weak ransom. The Leprechauns responded by harassing the kingdom each night—milking all the cows, making the wells dirty, and destroying the corn crop. The king ignored them until finally they threatened to shave the head of every single person in Ulster. King Fergus responded by assuring them he would kill Lubdan if they did such a thing to his people.

Lubdan called out of his window to the leprechauns and told them to fix everything they had ruined and go home. He turned to Fergus and told him he could choose a magical treasure for the ransom. The treasures included a spear that could fight off one hundred warriors, a cloak that would never age, a belt that would keep him healthy forever, or a caldron that could turn stone into delicious meat.

By this time, the little man Aedh had come back from Faylinn. He told the king it was a magical place where all the doors were made of gold. There were pillars made from crystal, and the columns were fashioned from silver. He explained to the king that the leprechauns were so small that he could fit seventeen maidens on his chest, and more could hide in his beard. Everywhere he had visited in the Kingdom of Faylinn, he had been hailed as a famous giant, which made him very pleased. He had loved his adventure to Faylinn.

King Fergus decided he would only accept King Lubdan's magical shoes in trade for freedom. The shoes allowed the wearer to travel underwater, under the lakes and the ocean. After that, Lubdan and Queen Bebo were free to leave, and they returned home to their kingdom.

Unfortunately, this gift led to the untimely death of King Fergus. The leprechauns had warned him to never go into Loch Ruadraige because a terrible monster called Muirdris lived within. The king didn't listen to this warning.

The monster rose from the loch and attacked King Fergus, disfiguring him. Everyone in the kingdom agreed not to tell the king that he was now hideous. They removed every mirror from the castle, and for seven years, King Fergus never saw his own reflection . . . until one fateful day.

A servant girl came to wash the king's hair, but he was in a terrible mood and struck at her with his whip. The girl was furious, so she showed Fergus his own reflection in the bowl of water. He was horrified at himself and immediately took off to the loch to slay the monster who had ruined his handsome face.

He used his sword, Caladbolg, and slayed the monster. Unfortunately, the wounds he received in the battle were just as bad as those of the monster. As he proclaimed himself the victor, he sank to the shore and died.

There are many more stories in the Ulster and Mythological Cycles about the leprechauns. In many of those stories, the leprechauns become increasingly mischievous and act as tricksters. In this story, however, they were merely curious and wanted to learn more about the human realm for the first time.

Merrow, the Irish Mermaid

A depiction of a mermaid at Clonfert Cathedral.
Andreas F. Borchert, CC BY-SA 3.0 DE <https://creativecommons.org/licenses/by-sa/3.0/de/deed.en>, via Wikimedia Commons;
https://commons.wikimedia.org/wiki/File:Clonfert_Cathedral_Mermaid_2009_09_17.jpg

The Irish mermaid is a fascinating form of the sidhe. Their Irish name is *murúch* (merrow), which is a form of the word "sea maid."

A merrow appears like the classic mermaid you are picturing, with a human body on top and a fish tail on the bottom. Her fish scales are green, and so is her hair, which she always loves to comb. Her top half is that of a very beautiful woman. However, the Irish merrow is unique. Each one has a special hat, or cap, they must wear to go between the deep waters and dry land. The cap is called *cochaillín draíochta*, which translates to "little magic hood."

Some folklore says the cap covers the merrow's entire body, while in a few tales from Scotland, merpeople have fish scales covering their skin instead of a lovely cap. Irish and Scottish folklore have a similar character, that of the selkie, who can shed her seal skin to shapeshift into a human or another creature.

Mermaids can be captured by human men, and they do sometimes marry into the human family. If an Irish mermaid marries a human man, he will take her *cochaillín draíochta* and hide it so she can't escape from him and return to the fairy realm. While she's missing her cap and dwelling on land, she will appear human-like in form, losing her tail.

There's just one thing that will give away her true sidhe mermaid status. She will always have a slight webbing between her fingers and toes, and so will any child she has with her human husband. She will always long to return to her home in the sea, and so will any of her offspring with human men.

There are also mermen in Irish folklore, though mermaids seem to be the most spoken of by human men who wish to capture one for themselves. The mermen are said to be hideous, ugly creatures, which is why mermaids often lurk above the waves, hoping to capture a human man.

Yes, it can work both ways. A man can capture a lovely mermaid and take her home to marry her on land, but a mermaid can also lure a handsome man below the sea and hold him captive in an enchanted state in her realm.

Merrow music, known as *samguba*, is hauntingly beautiful. It travels from the deepest, darkest part of the ocean some distance across the wind and waves. Merpeople love to dance to their music, both underwater and above on land. If a human isn't careful, they can become hypnotized to sleep by this lovely music and drown.

In the famous Book of Invasions, the Milesians encounter mermaids as siren-like creatures. Other ancient names for the merpeople include *murdúchann*, where "chann" refers to their siren song, *samguba*, and *suire*, which refers to the Milesians calling the merpeople sea nymphs. *Muirgheilt*, which means "sea-wanderer," is yet another name for them.

Maighdean mhara is the modern-day Irish term for sea maid, or mermaid.

Mermaid tales can also be found in the Ulster Cycle; for example, a mermaid is embedded in the tale "The Wooing of Emer."

The Púca or Pooka

In the United States, you may have heard reference to a pooka; in Ireland, they are referred to as púcas. These members of the sidhe are solitary in nature and represent a spirit or a ghost. Their tribe of sidhe is known by the plural form of the word, púcaí. They can bring good or bad luck to a human, having been known to help the weary traveler or sometimes lead them astray. The pooka has the power of human speech, which it uses for both good and bad.

The pooka can have green, black, or white fur like the fairy hound. In Irish myths, the pooka is a shapeshifter, taking the shape of animals such as a horse, cat, dog, rooster, goat, or hare. Occasionally, the pooka can shift into a human form, but it always has remnants of an animal visible, such as the ears or a tail.

Often the pooka appears as a sleek black horse with luminous golden eyes. The pooka will entice riders onto its back and then take them for the ride of their lives, tossing them to and fro. The pooka doesn't intend to do harm to the rider, luckily.

Legend has it that only one human man has ever been able to ride the pooka in horse form. That man is the last High King of Ireland, Brian Boru. He used three strands of the pooka's tail to create a magical bridle to control the fairy horse.

The pooka's day of the year is November 1. On this day, the pooka's role varies widely by region. In many areas, as the last of the harvest is brought in, a small amount is left behind for the pooka, as it's a hungry creature. The pooka dwells in the mountains and hills of Ireland. In those hilly areas on November 1, the pooka is said to appear and give advice, prophecies, and warnings to those who seek it out.

Pookas have appeared in various books, movies, and comics over the years. One pooka-like character that everyone will have heard of is the Cheshire Cat from *Alice in Wonderland*. This mischievous little creature is the perfect embodiment of the features a pooka has in Irish myths.

The Fairy Queen Áine

Áine, pronounced "On-ya," is the Irish goddess of summer, love, protection, fertility, wealth, and sovereignty. She's known as *Leanan Sidhe*, meaning "Sweetheart of the Sidhe," and Queen of the Fairies. She's one of the most beloved and powerful goddesses.

Áine is closely tied to the Hill of KnockÁiney, or Cnoc Áine, located in Munster, County Limerick.

Áine is most known for two things. She's regarded as the one who gave grain to all of Ireland because of one legend where she sat on her birthing chair and birthed a sheaf of grain. She's also well renowned for overcoming adversity and taking revenge on a man who committed wrongs against her, specifically a man named Ailill, who happened to be the king of Munster.

At the time of our story, King Ailill was feeling very anxious. The grass in his fields wouldn't grow well, meaning his livestock wouldn't have food. And if the livestock didn't eat, well then the people wouldn't be fed in turn.

Ferchess the Druid told the king to visit the Hill of KnockÁiney on Samhain Eve to find guidance from the enchanted place. Unfortunately, instead of solving his problems, he created a new one, as the weakness of his human spirit went up against a deity from the Otherworld.

King Ailill entered a lazy half-asleep, half-awake state once he reached the Hill of KnockÁiney. He was sleep-walking when he saw a shining vision. Before him was Áine, the daughter of Eoghabal of the Tuatha Dé Danann. She was so gorgeous that Ailill was filled with human desire. He forgot his dignity as the king and attacked her, raping her.

Áine was absolutely furious at the king for his actions. She immediately sought revenge, biting off the king's ear and leaving him maimed for the rest of his life.

As you may remember from previous stories, in Celtic tradition a leader cannot rule if they aren't in perfect physical condition. Remember King Nuada and the arm he lost at the Battle of Moytura, and how it was replaced by a bionic arm to make him perfect again so he could resume his role as king? When Áine bit off the king's ear, he was no longer perfect and fit to be the High King of Ireland. This was the perfect revenge.

After that day, King Ailill was known as King Ailill Aulom. Aulom means "one-eared." He was never able to reign over his kingdom again.

The descendants of King Ailill and Áine became known as the Eoghanachta. They established a strong dynasty that ruled over the southern half of Ireland. This contributed to the folklore claiming that Áine had the ability to grant power and sovereignty.

There are many other stories of Áine and her interactions with mortal men—notably, a story about Gerald, the Earl of Desmond, who stole her cloak while she was swimming in a river. He refused to return it until she married him. Their son, Gearóid Iarla, was a powerful magician. The story goes that Áine promised Gerald that his son would never surprise him, but when their son performed a superhuman act, Gerald was surprised. This freed Áine to return to the sidhe realm.

In the area of the Hill of KnockÁiney, the people used to celebrate Áine by lighting bales of hay on fire in midsummer and carrying them to the hilltop. From there, the burning bales would be sent down to fertilize the fields with their ashes. The last record of the straw bale ritual was in 1879.

There are also a number of stories telling of Áine appearing to people in the area dressed as a beggar lady. If the person was kind to her, she would repay them with blessings in return.

Sidhe in Popular Culture

The fairy realm is often thought of in modern culture as somewhere magical, with flowers and sparkling light. While this is correct for some aspects of the Otherworld, it's not fully accurate.

Tinkerbell helped shape Western ideas about the fairies, as did J.M. Barrie's Peter Pan character, who was not portrayed as a fairy but shares many similarities to sidhe, including arriving from an Otherworld and possessing magical abilities.

Fairy aesthetic (fairycore) is popular on social media, portraying them as ethereal creatures with pointy ears, luminous wings, and a strong connection to nature. What's left out is the rest of the fairy world. Creatures like the pooka, mermaid, leprechaun, and banshee are not understood to be part of the sidhe or the fairy races, as they are in true Irish mythology.

Perhaps this is another example of the appropriation of Irish culture, as a false idea of what makes up a fairy has been exploited and spread in popular culture. The commercialized concept of the pointy-eared fairy is *completely* lacking the rich, interwoven tapestry of folklore and oral storytelling that the Irish people so deeply treasure. The sidhe and their stories have been an integral part of Irish culture both in the past and in the present.

Chapter 5: The Four Cycles of Irish Mythology

It may sound strange to refer to cycles as a way to organize Irish mythology, but what that really means are periods of Irish history and their related stories, legends, folk tales, and myths. As introduced in Chapter 1, there are three main cycles of Irish mythology, with some scholars squeezing in a fourth cycle. From oldest to newest there is the Mythological Cycle, the Ulster Cycle, the Fenian Cycle, and Historical Cycle.

The ancient and early Irish peoples didn't divide any of their folklore into these cycles. The cycles were created by scholars who sought to organize Irish mythology into distinct groups. The sources for the stories in the cycles are found in three main books.

These cycles represent four separate, fully immersive worlds of Irish folklore. They each have separate characters, but the locations and themes overlap at times. If you read the stories carefully, you will catch glimpses of gods, goddesses, and kings from other cycles appearing in multiple places as background characters.

The Mythological Cycle

The Mythological Cycle is the most ancient of the four cycles, covering the fantastical stories of the earliest races and tribes to inhabit the island of Ireland. This includes the stories we have just discussed about the Tuatha Dé Danann, the Fir Bolg, the Fomorians, and the Milesians. These stories are all about the gods and goddesses and involve supernatural occurrences.

These stories are ancient, which means they are the least preserved of the four cycles. The basis for the stories are found in the *Metrical Dindshenchas,* or "Lore of Places," and the *Lebor Gabála Érenn,* or Book of Invasions. These stories were put on paper by Irish monks between the tenth and fourteenth centuries.

The Children of Lir is one of the most well-known stories from the Mythological Cycle. We will discuss that story in depth in the next chapter. In this tragic story, a stepmother is jealous of four children that she turned into swans.

The Wooing of Étain

The Wooing of Étain is another story from the Mythological Cycle that is famous in all of Ireland. In this story, M a powerful and handsome sidhe king, falls hopelessly in love with Étain, who is already married to the High King of Ireland. Midir attempts to woo Étain, but High King Eochaid becomes suspicious of Midir's advances. The High King decides to challenge Midir to a series of difficult, nearly impossible tasks. Miraculously, Midir manages to complete the tasks, but he is still rejected as Étain's lover.

Midir's wife, Fuamnach, is absolutely furious at this development. She sends a strong storm to batter the little fly, hoping to eradicate her. Unfortunately for Fuamnach, Étain blows through the window of a mortal king's hall, where she falls straight into the goblet of this king's wife. As the tale continues, Étain's sister is the mortal king's wife who accidentally swallows the little fly. She becomes pregnant instantly and gives birth to a lovely child, who is Étain reborn.

Midir recognizes Étain and falls in love with her all over again. Now Étain is the child of a mortal lord, and despite Midir trying everything he can to woo her, she is married off to the brother of High King Eochaid, named Ailill.

Eochaid recognizes his wife Étain and becomes jealous of his brother Ailill. A bitter love rectangle filled with jealousy develops between Midir, Ailill, Eochaid, and Étain. The story is full of drama and culminates in Midir challenging Eochoaid to a game of Fidchell, which is similar to chess. If Midir wins, he will get Étain for a day.

Midir does win the game of Fidchell, but Eochaid is so very jealous that he tries everything he can to intervene. Midir uses his fairy powers to whisk Étain away, taking her to his sidhe palace.

Eochaid is desperate to reclaim Étain, so he enlists the help of sorcerers and Druids. This sets the stage for an epic showdown between the mortal and fairy realms.

Étain cries out for peace, but Eochaid and Midir cannot stop themselves. Étain is transformed into a swan, who then flies far away, beyond the reach of the sidhe or any mortal men.

In an alternate ending of the tale, when Midir and Étain hug each other, they both transformed into swans, flying away together.

The name Étain in Gaelic means "jealousy." This story serves to remind the Irish people how jealous feuds can tear apart families and neighbors, with no one winning in the end—especially not the jealous person.

The Dream of Aengus

The Irish god of youth and love is known as Aengus. His name means the "chosen one" because *aon* means "one" and *gus* means "choice." His stories in the Mythological Cycle all involve love and passion.

The Dagda, the father god of the Tuatha Dé Danann, was Aengus' own father. Due to magical spells, Aengus was conceived and born on the very same day.

Aengus had musical talent, playing his magical harp that created an intense desire and attraction in everyone who heard it. It is said that fluttering birds represented the kisses of Aengus, and you could see four little birds always flying around his head. Some say those birds carried love messages for Aengus.

He was living in a state of perpetual youth, as a man in the prime of his young life, when he became lovesick over a beautiful sidhe fairy girl he could not find and only saw in his dreams.

The story of Aengus and his one true love, Caer Ibormeith, the goddess of sleep and dreams, goes as follows:

Aengus was laying in his bed, soundly sleeping one night, when he suddenly saw a vision that appeared to be the most beautiful woman in Eriu coming toward the head of his bed. He reached out for her and tried to take her hand so that he could pull her toward him, but she disappeared. Who had taken her from his arms? He laid in bed all night thinking about the vision he had seen. The stress from thinking about it made him sick. He couldn't eat all day.

Time went on, and soon a full year had gone by with this woman visiting him every night in bed but never speaking to him. Sometimes, she played him beautiful music on the timpán. He had fallen head over heels in love with her.

By this point, Aengus was quite sick since he hardly had any appetite, but no one could figure out what was wrong with him. He still hadn't told a soul about the nightly apparition. The town's doctor couldn't tell what was wrong with Aengus, so the doctor of Cond, Fergne, came to examine him. This doctor could tell just from a glimpse at a man's face what illness he had; he could even tell how many people were sick inside of a home based on the type of smoke coming out of their chimney.

Fergne spoke quietly to Aengus outside. He asked Aengus if he had become lovesick.

"Yes," Aengus confessed. He explained that the girl he saw in his bedroom was the most beautiful he had ever seen in his life.

Fergne told Aengus that he would send for his mother Boann so that she could speak with the lovesick man. (His mother Boann was the goddess after which the River Boyne has been named.)

When Boann arrived, Fergne explained what was ailing her son. He told Boann to tend to Aengus and search through Eriu until she found the lady her son had seen.

Boann carried out the search for this woman for a full year but never found her. She asked for Fergne to return. When he got there, Boann told him there was no help to be found for her son; they couldn't find this woman.

Fergne told her to send for the man's father, the Dagda. When the Dagda got to Eriu, he was annoyed that he had been summoned. He asked Boann why he had been called for, and she told him he needed to help his son. The Dagda was frustrated, saying he didn't know any more information than Boann.

The Dagda was king of the sidhe of Eriu. Boann wanted the Dagda to ask King Bodb, king of the sidhe of Mumu, to search his part of the sidhe for this woman. The family went to visit King Bodb, who happily promised to search for the woman in his kingdom for a year so that they could be certain if she was there.

After a year Bodb's search party came and told him they had found the girl at Loch Bél Dracon in Cruitt Cliach. Messengers were sent to the

Dagda, immediately requesting that Aengus return with them so he could be taken to meet the girl and confirm she was indeed the girl from his dreams.

Aengus rode in a chariot to Séd ar Femuin, the home of King Bodb. Aengus and the king's lords and ladies feasted there for three days and three nights. Then, Bodb asked Aengus if he was ready to go see the girl. King Bodb told Aengus that he could meet the girl, but the king had no power to give her to him.

They traveled until they reached a large lake. At the lake, there were one hundred and fifty girls. Aengus saw his girl among them. The other girls only came up to her shoulders in height. She wore a silver necklace, and her hair chain was made of gold.

The king told Aengus he could do no more to help him. The girl was Cáer Ibormeith, daughter of Ethal Anbúail from Síd Uamuin in the province of Connachta.

Aengus and King Bodb returned back to Aengus' home in Eriu. They gave the news to Boann and the Dagda. Aengus was crushed that he couldn't get to the girl. Bodb suggested that the Dagda should contact Ailill and Maeve, since they were the king and queen over the land where the girl lived.

So, the Dagda did just that, taking with him three score of chariots. The king and queen were pleased to see him and spent a full week enjoying a feast with him in the banquet hall. During the week of feasting, the Dagda explained to King Ailill why he had come. He told Dagda that his son had fallen in love with a girl in the kingdom and was now lovesick and pining away for her.

The king and queen told the Dagda that they did not have the power to give the girl to Aengus. They told the Dagda to summon the king of the sidhe. Meanwhile, King Ailill sent a messenger to the girl's father, Ethal Anbúail, requesting that he come to speak to King Ailill and Queen Maeve. He refused, saying that he would not give his daughter to the son of the Dagda.

When Ailill heard this news, he said that it didn't matter. The man would be forced to come, and Ailill would also take the heads of the man's warriors for his disrespect. King Ailill's people and the Dagda's people destroyed the warriors of Ethal Anbúail and took three score's worth of heads, trapping Ethal Anbúail in Crúachu. King Ailill confronted Ethal Anbúail and demanded he hand over his daughter for Aengus.

Ethal Anbúail said it wasn't in his power to give his daughter away because she was more powerful than he was. Ailill was surprised. Her power was the ability to shapeshift. For one year, she would be a bird, then spend the following year as a human, switching between the two forms every other year.

Ailill demanded to know when the girl would next be a bird, but Ethal Anbúail refused to say until King Ailill threatened to remove his head also. Finally, Ethal Anbúail confessed that his daughter would become a bird next Samhain at Loch Bél Dracon, the Lake of the Dragon's Mouth, with one hundred and fifty other swans. The three made peace with each other and went their separate ways. The Dagda took the news home to his son, telling him to go to Loch Bél Dracon next Samhain and call for his beloved.

Finally, when Samhain arrived, Aengus traveled to Loch Bél Dracon and called out to her. She called back, telling him she would only speak with him if he promised she would be able to return to the water. He promised, and she flew to him. As they embraced, Aengus turned into a swan as well. They held each other and slept as swans until they had gone around the lake three times together. They flew away from the lake together as swans, going to Brú na Bóinne, the Newgrange Mound in Boyne. As they flew, sweet fairy music followed behind them. Their beautiful song was so powerful that the people of Boyne slept for three days and three nights.

Aengus remained with his girl forever, since swans mate for life. The god of love and youth had found his own one true love.

You'll notice several important themes in this legend that repeat themselves throughout the Mythological Cycle, as well as in other parts of Irish folklore. The swans represent more than just a connection with nature. Swans mate for life, making them a perfect symbol of fidelity and love. They are prominent characters in other stories from the Mythological Cycle, including The Children of Lir.

The number three also plays an important role throughout this story. The swans swam around the lake three times together. Aengus feasted with King Ailill for three days and three nights. The people of Boyne slept after hearing Caer's fairy music for three days and three nights.

As you may remember, three was a holy number for the Celts, symbolizing birth, death, and renewal. This is the full cycle of life, as Celts believe the soul never dies, it just passes through the different cycles.

The Dream of Aengus is both a love story and a tale of determination. It does leave us with a few questions, as many myths do. Why did Caer, the goddess of sleep and dreams, appear to Aengus in the first place? Why did she make herself so difficult to find? Do you think this was a test, to see if Aengus truly loved her enough to seek her out and keep his promise to allow her to return to the water?

The Ulster Cycle

The change between the Mythological Cycle and the Ulster Cycle was marked by a distinct shift between magical beings and settlers to stories of war. This cycle features warriors, the sorrows of war, and depicts battles. The stories concentrate on the House of the Red Branch, a military order.

Clues from history lead scholars to believe that the stories from the Ulster Cycle are largely based in Iron Age. The main part of the Ulster Cycle was set during the reign of Conchobar in Ulster and Queen Medb (Maeve) in Connacht. They ruled two neighboring kingdoms, which were similar to two states. Conchobar's death coincides with the day Christ was crucified.

The Hound of Culann

The main character in these stories is Cú Chulainn, who is considered the greatest hero in all Celtic myths. Cú Chulainn's given name is Sétanta. He was the son of the god Lugh and Dechtire, the sister of King Conchobar. The story of how Cú Chulainn became Sétanta's nickname is famous across all of Ireland. It goes something like this:

One evening, King Conchobar went with his fellow warriors to have dinner with a friend named Culann. The king was raising Sétanta as his son, and he invited the young boy to come along for the dinner. Sétanta told the king he would rather play hurley, a game similar to hockey. He promised the king he would show up later, once he was done playing.

Culann was a wealthy man with a mansion on a large piece of property in a place called Quelgny. Each night, Culann would let his best hound run loose around his home as a guard dog. This hound was fearsome and deadly, a crazy beast that would kill attempted robbers that might try to sneak up on Culann and his family.

The king and Culann had forgotten all about Sétanta until they heard Culann's terrifying guard hound baying outside. Everyone at the dinner table heard the terrifying noises of fighting. Fearing the worst for Sétanta, all the men in the mansion ran outside. To their shock, they found Sétanta standing over the dead dog. Sétanta had killed the guard dog with his hurley stick.

The king praised Sétanta for his bravery and skill, but Culann was understandably distraught at the death of his best guard dog. Sétanta promised Culann that he would guard the property himself with a spear and shield for a year. Meanwhile, he would train a pup from the dead hound to be an even better guard dog. After this fateful night, Sétanta earned his nickname Cú Chulainn, the Hound of Culann.

Donn Cúailnge

The second infamous story starring Cú Chulainn is called Donn Cúailnge. The original story can be found in *Lebor na hUidre* (The Book of the Dun Cow) and *Lebor Buide Lecáin* (The Yellow Book of Lecan).

This is a story about the Brown Bull of Cooley, an extremely fertile stud bull. This bull caused an epic battle known as The Cattle Raid of Cooley, or *Táin Bó Cúailnge*, a hallmark story in the Ulster Cycle.

The beginning of the Brown Bull of Cooley saga starts with two men. They were each pig keepers. One worked for the king of the Munster sidhe, and the other worked for the king of the Connaught sidhe. The two men were in constant opposition. The people of the area found out they could transform themselves into different forms and constantly pit them against each other to see who had the greatest powers.

First, they cursed each other's pigs, putting a spell on the pigs so that they would eat but always remain lean. This got them both fired by their masters but showed that their powers were equal.

Next, their non-stop squabbling began. They changed into birds and fought with each other for two years. They fought as sea creatures in the river, and they fought as stags and destroyed each other's homes. They changed into two human warriors, attacking each other in bloody fights. They were two phantoms, each trying to scare the other to death. They became two dragons, each trying to freeze the other by burying their opponent's land in snow.

Somehow, in a course of unfortunate events, they chose to fight as two worms and were swallowed by separate cows. The men were reborn in the form of bulls. One bull was Donn Cúailnge, the brown bull. The other was Finnbhennach, meaning "white-horned."

Donn belonged to the cattle lord of Ulster's herd. The white-horned bull belonged to the herd of Queen Medb. The white-horned bull realized he belonged to a woman and considered that beneath him, so he instead joined the herd of her husband, King Ailill.

When Queen Medb discovered that Ailill owning the white-horned bull made her husband richer than she was, she was determined to own the powerful brown bull Donn Cúailnge to boost her prestige.

First, Queen Medb decided to diplomatically acquire the brown bull. She sent a friendly message to the owner, Dáire. She offered him riches of land and treasure or even sexual favors if he desired. She asked to possess the bull for one year. Dáire accepted her offer and was all set to send the bull to Medb when things went awry. The messenger became drunk and began boasting that Queen Medb would have taken the bull by force if Dáire had not agreed to the diplomatic trade. This made Dáire angry, and he withdrew his acceptance of the queen's offer.

Queen Medb gathered an army and sent it to march on Dáire to take the bull by force. Fergus mac Róich led the army. The Mórrígan assumed the form of a crow and flew ahead, warning the brown bull of the coming army. The bull then went on a rampage.

The men of Ulster wanted to fight Queen Medb's army but were disabled by a terrible curse. The only warrior who wasn't affected by the curse was Cú Chulainn, due to his young age. Instead of watching the border for the approaching army, Cú Chulainn was distracted by a tryst, and Queen Medb's men managed to find Donn Cúailnge, the brown bull.

Donn Cúailnge gored the first herdsmen who tried to grab him. He created a stampede with fifty of his heifers, trampling over fifty men in the army, before the herd took off into the countryside, leaving Queen Medb's men in the dust.

Cú Chulainn joined the fight, meeting the queen's army at Mount Slieve Foy. Here, Cú Chulainn invoked the right of single combat at a river ford. The one-on-one battles raged on for months as Cú Chulainn continued to defeat each champion.

While Cú Chulainn was distracted, the brown bull, Donn Cúailnge, was captured elsewhere, along with twenty-four cows. Cú Chulainn showed up, killing the twenty-four cows and other men, but in the fray Donn Cúailnge ran away again.

Finally, a battle between Queen Medb's army and the Ulster warriors ended with the queen's men retreating. However, the queen was somehow able to capture Donn Cúailnge. He fought with Finnbhennach, the white-horned bull, to finish their initial argument that had started in human form.

The fight was long and bloody. In the end, the brown bull won, and the white bull was dead. Unfortunately, the brown bull was also mortally wounded. He hobbled around the countryside, leaving behind multiple places that would be named after him, before returning to Cooley to die.

The Fenian Cycle

The Fenian Cycle was written down in the third century CE. This cycle features Munster, Leinster, and Scotland prominently. The Fenian Cycle is known for Fianna lore. The Fenians were a nomadic people who loved to hunt and fight. The stories feature warriors and heroes, though this cycle moves away from just war stories and more toward romance. Animals appear as magical beings that bring wisdom and knowledge.

The famous story The Salmon of Knowledge is in this cycle. This kicks off a long section of mythology related to Fionn mac Cumhaill.

The Salmon of Knowledge

As the tale goes, in the River Boyne, there was a salmon called the Salmon of Knowledge. The first person to eat this fish would be granted wisdom over all other men. A poet named Finegas lived near this river. He had been trying for several years to catch this special fish. He was already known as one of the wisest men in all of Ireland.

A young warrior by the name of Fionn mac Cumhaill (Finn McCool) came to live with Finegas. Fionn had no idea about the existence of the Salmon of Knowledge. Fionn always asked Finegas why he spent all of his time fishing, but Finegas would only smile in response, never giving an actual answer.

One morning, Fionn heard shouting from the riverbank. Finegas had managed to catch a large salmon. The fish glimmered silver, brighter than other fish in the river. Finegas immediately realized that he had finally captured the Salmon of Knowledge!

Finegas had exhausted himself catching the fish and wrestling it onto the riverbank. He asked Fionn if he might cook the fish for him but warned Fionn not to taste even a single morsel of the fish's flesh. Fionn was glad to help Finegas, so he cooked the fish over the fire. As he was turning the fish, he accidentally burned his thumb on the hot skin. Letting out a yelp of pain, Fionn put his thumb into his mouth to cool his burning finger as an automatic reaction.

Shortly after, Fionn brought the cooked fish to Finegas. It was then that Finegas gazed into Fionn's eyes. He could see that there was something different about Fionn now. Finegas asked Fionn if he had eaten any of the salmon. Fionn insisted he had not. Then, Fionn remembered burning his thumb and placing it in his mouth.

Finegas was saddened because he knew Fionn had gained the wisdom from the Salmon of Knowledge. Finegas would never be the wisest man in Ireland now. However, Finegas was not a selfish man. He was happy for Fionn.

Shortly after becoming the wisest man in Ireland, Fionn left the home of Finegas. He became the leader of the Fianna and is now known as the greatest warrior Ireland has ever had.

The Goblin

One of Fionn mac Cumhaill's other famous adventures tells of what happened after Fionn left Finegas. Full of wisdom, he challenged an evil goblin who would terrorize the people living on the Hill of Tara every Samhain. This goblin was named Aillén mac Midgna.

The goblin would set fire to buildings and perform other evil deeds. No warriors could challenge this goblin because he had a magical harp. Music from the harp would put even the most powerful warrior right to sleep.

Finally, one Samhain, Fionn stood before the Fianna and pledged to kill the goblin. His only request was that if he were successful on his quest, he would be made the leader of the Fianna, like his father before him.

The king agreed, and a friend of Fionn's father gave Fionn a magic spear. He told Fionn to press the spear against his forehead when the goblin began to play the enchanting harp music to keep himself awake.

As night fell, Fionn heard the fairy music coming from a distance. He held the spear against his forehead and waited. Soon, the goblin crept closer. Suddenly, Fionn threw the spear, striking the goblin through the heart. The goblin vanished into a cloud of mist.

Fionn returned to the king, where the king proclaimed him the next leader of the Fianna. From there, Fionn ruled the Fianna out of his fort on the Hill of Allen in County Kildare.

Oisín

Sometimes this cycle is also called the Ossianic Cycle because it was supposedly written by Oisín. This is the same Oisín we spoke of before, who was in love with the goddess Niamh and went to live in Tír na nÓg.

When telling the story of Oisín and Niamh in the previous chapter, the history of Oisín was left out. Oisín is the son of the infamous Fionn mac Cumhaill, who consumed the Salmon of Knowledge.

How Oisín came to be is a tale in its own right.

As the legend goes, a young maiden with the name Sadhbh refuses the amorous advances of an older Druid named Dorcha. As punishment, she is changed into a deer. A short time later, the famous hounds of Fionn mac Cumhaill, Bran and Sceolan, were running ahead of their owner while out hunting. They come across this deer under a rowan tree.

As Fionn catches up to his dogs, he sees them sniffing around the deer. It's immediately obvious there is something unique about this deer. To Fionn's surprise the deer transforms into a lovely young woman. She tells them her name is Blaith Dearg, the daughter of Finn's greatest enemy, Dearg.

Blaith invites Fionn to spend the night with her, as she found him far more appealing than the older Druid man she had been promised to. When Fionn wakes up the next morning, Blaith has vanished.

About a year later, Fionn passes by the same rowan tree. To his shock, there in the same spot where he had met Blaith Dearg, a baby sits. He knows this is Blaith's baby that he had fathered during their one night together. Fionn takes the baby and names him Oisín.

Oisín grows into a striking young man. He is able to pass every rigorous test to be allowed to join the Fianna with great ease. Oisín is well loved by the Fianna and his father, and he becomes famous throughout the region as a warrior and a poet.

One day, Oisín is sitting on a bench at sunrise, when the glimmering first light of day suddenly transforms into a beautiful woman with golden hair named Niamh. From there, the well-known love story of Oisín and Niamh begins, as he accepts her invitation to travel back to Tír na nÓg on the back of her white horse Embarr. He marries and lives with her for the following three hundred years.

The King Cycle

The King Cycle is also known as the Historical Cycle. The tales in this cycle are all about kingship, wars between kings, and marriages between kings and goddesses or realms. The goddesses often represented a king's relationship with the land. The stories in this cycle tell what it means to be a good king and how to bring prosperity to the kingdom, giving examples of both successful kings and unsuccessful kings from middle and old Irish literature. Most of the tales are told in a poetic style, as they were recited by bards.

Many of the kings found in these stories are considered semi-historical figures. Some aren't historically proven to have existed, while others have been shown to represent actual kings. Some include Cormac mac Airt, Conaire Mor, Niall of the Nine Hostages, Labhraidh Loingseach, and Mongan.

The most popular story in this cycle is *Buile Shuibhne*, The Frenzy of Sweeny (or The Madness of Sweeney). The story tells the tale of Duibhne of the Dál Riada (or Riata), who was injured in battle. He then roamed through Ireland's wildest places desperately searching for peace.

Symbolism, Overlap, and Relevance Today

In the following chapters, we also want to examine the role of the cycles in shaping Irish storytelling traditions and the ongoing legacy of these cycles in contemporary Irish culture. Why are these cycles important? Are they still important in the modern day?

Chapter 6: The Children of Lir

As mentioned earlier, the best known story from the Mythological Cycle is the Children of Lir.

LÊR AND THE SWANS
From the Drawing by J. H. Bacon, A.R.A.

Lir and his swan children.
https://commons.wikimedia.org/wiki/File:Ler_swans_Millar.jpg

The story goes like this.

Long, long ago in the realm of the Tuatha Dé Danann, King Dagda died.

As the council gathered to choose a new king, the sea god Lir expected to be next in line for the throne. Alas, he wasn't chosen. Instead, Bodb Dearg became king. Lir was furiously angry and stormed away, refusing to accept the new king.

Wanting to win Lir's favor, Dearg gave Lir his daughter Aoibha (Eva) in marriage. Lir and his wife lived with their four lovely children in their castle and had a happy life. The children were named Fionnula, Aodh, Conn and Fiachra.

Sadly, Aoibha died. Lir and his children pined for her, missing her every moment of every day. The king wanted his children to have a mother to care for them, and the children's grandfather King Dearg was also grief-stricken and wanted to help the family. So, it was decided that Lir would remarry.

Dearg offered his daughter Aoife to be Lir's new wife. At first, everything was going well. Aoife was beautiful, but time revealed that her inner beauty did not match her outer beauty. Her heart wasn't pure.

In the beginning, Aoife adored Lir's four children. Unfortunately, as time went on she began to grow jealous of them as she realized they would always take precedence over her when it came to Lir's affection. Aoife decided that she wanted the king all for herself, so she made a plan to get rid of the children.

One warm summer's day, Aoife offered to take the children swimming in Lough Derravaragh. The children were swimming without any worries, enjoying the day. When they weren't paying attention, Aoife pulled out a Druid's wand. She cast a spell on the children. In an instant, there was a blinding flash of light, and all four children disappeared. Where the children had been there were four majestic swans with feathers as pure white as fresh-fallen snow.

There was a stunned silence as the confused swans swam in circles. Then, one of the swans opened its beak and spoke in Fionnula's voice.

"What have you done to us?" she asked. Aoife was pleased that her plan had worked flawlessly. A cackle escaped her lips as she answered, "The four of you will be swans for nine hundred years. Three hundred of those years will be spent at this lake, three hundred in the Sea of Moyle, and three hundred at Inish Glora. The only way this spell can be broken is with the ringing of a church bell."

At the end of the day, Lir was worried when his children didn't return home from swimming. He went down to the lake to find them, but all he saw were four swans. As he stood staring at the water, looking for any signs of his missing family, one of the swans opened its mouth and spoke in the voice of his daughter Fionnula.

Fionnula explained what Aoife had done. Lir rushed back to the castle and pleaded with Aoife to reverse the spell she had cast, but she refused. Lir banished her from the kingdom. When her father King Dearg found out what his daughter had done, he made her transform into an air demon, and as legend has it, she still remains in that form today.

Lir began spending all of his time down by the lake, listening to his children sing and watching them swim. Dearg also frequently joined Lir on the banks of the lake, listening to his grandchildren sing and offering support for Lir in a difficult time. His children watched helplessly as Lir grew older and died, breaking their hearts.

After three hundred years, they moved to the cold, windy Sea of Moyle between Ireland and Scotland. They much preferred the warm island where food was plentiful. By the time three hundred more years had passed and it was time to fly to Inish Glora, the swans had grown very old.

Finally, one morning at Inish Glora, the swans heard the sound they'd been longing for year after year. It was the sound of a Christian church bell ringing. The swans hurried to shore. As they made their way to the church, they began to change from birds to old people. The monk ringing the church bell was named Caomhog. He was shocked to see the swans morphing into humans right in front of him.

The children were now nine hundred years old, unable to live any longer on the human plane. The monk baptized them and listened to their life story. Soon after, when they died, he buried them together in one grave. That night, he vividly dreamed he saw four children flying above his head, through the clouds. He felt at peace knowing the children were finally reunited with their mother and father.

The Children of Lir incorporates similar motifs as many tales from the Mythological Cycle. We find jealousy as a main motive in the story. Dark magic is used against others. Sorrow is the end result; no one wins.

Manannán Mac Lir, the god of the sea, means "son of Lir" in Gaelic. This would make the four children the half-siblings of the famous

Manannán.

Manannán had such a strong influence on Irish folklore that he appeared in some form in all four cycles of Irish mythology.

Bodb Dearg was an excellent example of a wise and caring king. Bodb Dearg appeared in numerous other stories, including the Dream of Aengus featured in the Mythological Cycle. If you remember, the beautiful maiden Aengus saw was a maiden who transformed into a swan, just like the children of Lir.

Swans became symbols of love and fidelity throughout Ireland. Swans mate for life, which makes them a perfect symbol of true love. They are also said to represent transparency and purity. Lir showed unconditional love to his children, and Aengus pledged fidelity and love to his maiden, even turning into a swan himself so that they could fly away together. Swans were also a part of the Wooing of Étain.

The characters in the Children of Lir can mainly be found in two cycles of Irish mythology: the Mythological Cycle, of which this story is a part of, and the Ulster Cycle. The evil stepmother in the Children of Lir, Aoife, appears in the Ulster Cycle as a warrior. It's revealed that she was actually the foster daughter of King Dearg. Her real father was Ailill, the great warrior.

Matching up with the historical timeline, this story obviously incorporates the arrival of Christian monks in Ireland and shows how the people were beginning to blend the two worldviews into one, as both dark Druid magic and being baptized appear in the same tale.

Throughout history, the Children of Lir has become incorporated into all Irish culture. Numerous art, sculptures, and glass pieces have been created based on the folktale. Both classical and modern songs have been written based on the story. It's also referenced countless times in novels, poetry, and other literary works.

Interestingly, the Children of Lir has become a popular modern Irish jewelry piece. Intertwining white swans representing Lir's children are worn as a tribute to their memory.

People don't agree on the morals of the story. Is it about loyalty to the ones you love? Is it about the evils of jealousy and how one jealous person can alter the destiny of others? Or is it a story meant to teach us that we need to try to make the best of difficult situations that we can't change?

Regardless, the Children of Lir serves to bring together the Irish people with a common cultural bond. It's a tale that is both somber and magical, the perfect example of an Irish myth. The Children of Lir is a legend that will always live on in Irish culture, no matter how many years pass by. Swans dot the landscape and waterways of Ireland, serving as a constant reminder of the myth.

Chapter 7: Fionn mac Cumhaill and the Fianna

An illustration of Fionn mac Cumhaill.
Internet Archive Book Images, No restrictions, via Wikimedia Commons;
https://commons.wikimedia.org/wiki/File:Heroes_of_the_dawn_(1914)_(14566385007).jpg

Fionn mac Cumhaill, known colloquially as Finn McCool, is one of the most famous characters in Irish mythology. He was wise beyond his years, as we read in the Salmon of Knowledge. In the Hound of Culann, we heard of his intelligence and strength as a young boy when he defeated the fearsome guard hound.

The stories of Finn McCool are numerous. They were first shared as part of the oral tradition of Irish myths and eventually written down in the Fenian Cycle of Irish literature.

Finn McCool represents everything important about Irish culture. He is wise. He is brave, and he has a deep, enduring connection with the natural world.

Finn's father was Cumhaill, the powerful leader of the Fianna. His mother was Muirne, daughter of the Druid Tadg mac Nuadat. Finn's birth was itself dramatic, with prophecies and drama, starting out Finn McCool's life of extraordinary abilities and adventures with a bang right from conception.

When Finn was young, his father was killed by Goll mac Morna. To keep Finn safe from his father's enemies, he was hidden away deep in the forest. This time in his early life spent in the forest gave Finn his appreciation for nature and helped hone his character. He was raised in the woods as a skilled hunter, poet, and, most of all, a warrior.

After leaving the forest, Finn went to stay with the poet Finegas. As we learned in the last chapter, Finn managed to taste the Salmon of Knowledge. This shimmery fish was said to possess all of the world's wisdom. From this moment, Finn transformed from a warrior boy to a wise leader.

It was after this that Finn went on to win the right to be leader of the Fianna when he defeated a terrible Goblin named Aillén mac Midgna. Finn reclaimed his family's position from Goll mac Morna, the man who had killed his father.

Finn and his wisdom brought good qualities to the Fianna, including bravery, chivalry, and loyalty. Each story about Finn and the Fianna features Finn as the hero in fierce battles against supernatural beings. The stories usually center around lessons of bravery, love, betrayal, or friendship.

Finn McCool is indeed a character with heroic qualities, but in addition to that, he's portrayed as a giant in some versions of his legends. Scholars believe that Finn wasn't actually a giant in stature, but perhaps he was a symbolic giant. His status within the mythos was impressive, and his qualities were magnanimous.

The very landscape of Ireland is filled with Finn McCool. Geographical landmarks all over Ireland bear his legacy. Some of these include the Giant's Causeway, Lough Neagh, and the Isle of Mann. This strange and wonderful mixture of mythology and reality that creates the backbone of Irish culture can be clearly seen when looking for signs of Finn McCool in present-day Ireland. He serves as an enduring symbol of Ireland, forever shaping both the countryside's geography and the hearts of the people.

Have you ever seen the Giant's Causeway? This is a natural wonder, not something man-made. You can find it in County Antrim, Northern Ireland. Legend has it Finn McCool himself constructed the causeway so he could step across the North Channel to meet a Scottish giant named Benandonner. Stepping stones in the North Channel were a wise solution to complete Finn's journey.

At first, Finn didn't realize just how large the giant was. Startled by Benandonner's size, Finn and his wife came up with a way to trick the giant. They would pretend that Finn was a massive baby rather than an adult. His wife dressed him up as a baby, and when Benandonner arrived at Finn's home, his wife told him to be quiet so as not to wake her sleeping baby.

When Benandonner saw the massive "baby," he was frightened and terrified. If Finn's baby was that large, how much larger would his father Finn be? The giant ran back across the Giant's Causeway, smashing it as he thundered through.

We can clearly see Finn's bravery, wisdom, and determination play out in this tale. It also shows how the myths of the gods and goddesses explained creation and landmarks to the ancient Irish people.

The largest lake in the British Isles is known as Lough Neagh. The explanation for the formation of this large lake lies quite literally in the palm of Finn McCool. According to the legend, Finn scooped up a huge piece of earth when he was filled with rage.

He threw the chunk of earth at his Scottish rival across the sea. The earth ball missed Finn's Scottish rival and instead it landed in the Irish Sea, where it became the Isle of Man. The crater left behind by the removed earth turned into Lough Neagh when it filled up with water.

While the Fenian Cycle is primarily based on the heroic life of Finn McCool, quite a bit of the poetry was written by Finn's son, Oisín. This is the same Oisín who fell deeply in love with Niamh. These poems and stories were written down in the medieval times.

"The Book of Leinster" and "The Book of the Dun Cow," which both talk about Finn McCool, are two of the most famous books from the Fenian Cycle. These two books contain some of the most important insights we have into ancient Irish culture. Many of the stories include Oisín as an older man, remembering the amazing golden age of the Fianna and his father Finn McCool.

Finn's impact was so long-lasting that political parties have even named themselves after him. The Fenians, an 1800s group who sought freedom from the United Kingdom, named themselves after the heroic Finn and his band of warriors.

Today, one of Ireland's top political parties is called the Fianna Fáil. *Fianna* still means warrior in Irish today. The name of the party translates to "Soldiers of Destiny," with a nod to the ultimate Irish soldier and his warriors: Finn McCool and the Fianna.

Chapter 8: The Mórrígan

Do you remember Danu, the goddess of the Tuatha Dé Danann? Well, the Tuatha Dé Danann had more than one goddess figure. Another important goddess in the Mythological and Ulster Cycles is the Mórrígan.

As part of the Tuatha Dé Danann, the Mórrígan possessed magical powers. Her role in the myths always centered around the use of magic. The Mórrígan was the goddess of war, death, and fate in all of Celtic mythology. The Mórrígan is an earth goddess, connected with the fertility of the land and the breeding of cattle. She could also control water, including lakes, rivers, oceans, and all types of freshwater.

The Mórrígan is a sexual goddess, as well. She sleeps with gods or heroes, which ensures their victory in war.

The origins of the goddess Mórrígan are unclear. No one agrees on where she came from or who exactly she was, except that she was most certainly part of the Tuatha Dé Danann. The Mórrígan had multiple siblings, including Macha, Eriu, Banba, Badb, and Fohla. We know that her mother's name was Ernmas, another goddess of the Tuatha Dé Danann.

The Mórrígan's name is also a subject of interest and speculation among scholars. Morrigan, without the accent on the *o*, is an Old Irish spelling of the goddess's name and likely means "Nightmare Queen." Mórrígan and Mór-Ríoghain are both later Irish spellings. They are thought to mean "Great Queen." Other interpretations are "Queen of Phantoms," "Queen of the Slain," and "Sea Queen."

Most folklore agree that the Mórrígan was a very beautiful young woman with flawless, flowing dark hair. She wore a black cloak that often hid her face.

She could shapeshift into whatever form she wanted. Most of the time, the Mórrígan preferred to be in the form of a wolf or a crow. It makes sense that the Mórrígan would be represented by a crow, or sometimes a vulture. When anything dies in a field (for example, a cow in the herd or men in battle), the first thing to appear is always a hungry carrion bird. We can assume the Irish people saw this and associated the figure of the Mórrígan with the birds.

She had the tendency to be very frightening. If you look at the closely, you'll realize that while the Mórrígan can be a terrifying figure, she doesn't ever kill anyone. Crows don't kill people, either. Crows help hasten the decay process by eating and transforming dead bodies. The Mórrígan isn't Death itself; she is simply the keeper of death.

She seemed to have control over war and victory in battle. The Mórrígan would change into a crow and hover over the battlefields, manipulating the outcome. Afterward, the Mórrígan would claim the souls of those who died in the battle as a trophy.

Did you know the Mórrígan fell in love with Cú Chulainn, our brave warrior who defeated the hound? In the story The Myth of Cú Chulainn, the Mórrígan tries multiple times to seduce him but continually fails.

The Mórrígan could never accept that Cú Chulainn had rejected her, so she made plans to get revenge. The first attempt she made against Cú Chulainn was to redirect his path and confuse him. She changed into the shape of a bull, but Cú Chulainn ignored her and the plan failed. The second attempt the Mórrígan made was to trip Cú Chulainn. Once he tripped and fell, she would get closer to him to gain more strength, then use magic on him. She failed a second time. The Mórrígan's third attempt was in the form of a wolf. She wanted to scare Cú Chulainn. This also failed.

At this point, the Mórrígan had been injured several times in her animal forms, so she decided to try a different tactic. The Mórrígan changed into a human form. She became an old woman who pretended her only job was to milk the cows. Cú Chulainn was exhausted from the Mórrígan's previous attempts to trick him, and he didn't recognize her as a human. She offered him a drink of milk from one of her cows, and he gratefully accepted, blessing the Mórrígan for sharing milk. This blessing restored the Mórrígan to her full health, and she grew even stronger than she had been previously.

The Mórrígan felt an absolute surge of rage at her failures to trick Cú Chulainn. She decided that the only option at this juncture was for Cú Chulainn to die. One day shortly thereafter, Cú Chulainn was roaming around on his horse when he stumbled upon the Mórrígan, looking like a banshee and washing her bloody armor by the river. At this moment, Cú Chulainn knew he was going to die.

During the next battle, Cú Chulainn fought like a powerful hero. He became mortally wounded, and he knew these were his last few moments on the mortal plane. But Cú Chulainn had a plan. He managed to find a heavy rock and tie it to his body so that, when he died, he would remain sitting upright. He had already died when a crow landed on his shoulder and called out to inform the other soldiers of his death. No one could believe that the great Cú Chulainn was gone.

The Mórrígan is known as a triple goddess. Some scholars and folklore describe her as three sisters known as "The Three Morrígna." The three sisters are named Badb, Macha, and the Mórrígan, who is sometimes referred to as Anand or Nemain.

In Newgrange, Ireland, there is a grand, megalithic tomb-shrine possibly belonging to the Mórrígan. The tomb is centered around the number three, which, as we've discussed, is an important number in Celtic mythology and also represents the Mórrígan's triple goddess status.

Construction of the site at Newgrange began between 3200 and 3000 BCE and was not completed until 2,000 CE. It predates the pyramids at Giza and Stonehenge by some five hundred years. The Newgrange site contains a lightbox where the first rays of the sun hit on December 21, the Winter Solstice, and travel along the pathway that leads to the central burial chamber. The entire burial chamber is lit by this light for several moments, including a large triple spiral.

Inside the tomb, there are three stone cells. There are three stone basins with carvings of triplicate snake spirals. The Mórrígan is represented by the chevron, the inverted *V*, which is the earth element. The Mórrígan is considered the source of triple power. She's needed to take someone from birth to death and from death back to life. The figurines portray the female body as the passageway to life, with sprouting seeds and vulvas as a representation.

Figures like the Mórrígan often represent channels to the control of land, power, and fertility in Irish mythology. The Mórrígan has many ties to the landscape of Ireland, as noted in the Dindshenchas, which tells how places in Ireland earned their name.

Have you ever read Shakespeare's play *Macbeth*? In the opening scene, there are three old hags sitting around a fire, stirring a caldron and creating a spell that will bring death and sorrow to the characters in the play. The Mórrígan and her sisters were known to change into old hags, and this was clearly a representation of the Mórrígan as a triple goddess in *Macbeth*. The scene unfolds as follows:

ACT I

SCENE I. A desert place.

Thunder and lightning. Enter three Witches

First Witch

When shall we three meet again

In thunder, lightning, or in rain?

Second Witch

When the hurlyburly's done,

When the battle's lost and won.

Third Witch

That will be ere the set of sun.

First Witch

Where the place?

Second Witch

Upon the heath.

Third Witch

There to meet with Macbeth.

ALL

Fair is foul, and foul is fair:

Hover through the fog and filthy air.

Can you see the clear references to the triple goddess, the Mórrígan, in this opening passage? They even mention the battlefield and hovering through fog and filthy air.

Examining other popular stories, you might find references and characters based on the Mórrígan if you look carefully. The Mórrígan has appeared in Marvel Comics. She's also a video game character in both *Darkstalkers* and the *Dragon Age* series.

Chapter 9: The Banshee

An illustration of the banshee.
https://commons.wikimedia.org/wiki/File:Banshee.jpg

Do you know what the banshee is?

Many of us know of the mythological creature simply as something terrifying that shrieks. Often, the banshee is associated with evil because of the relationship with death, but in Irish mythology, the banshee isn't always bad. In fact, the true legend and mythology of the banshee has been largely misunderstood.

The Mórrígan and the banshee share similar qualities and are often confused. They can both shapeshift, often into a crow. They foretell death and are often seen at the scene of a battle. They've both been seen in the guise of an old woman, washing the clothing of a person who was about to die on a stone in the river. In folklore, like the Mórrígan, the banshee was also tasked with gathering and guiding souls. Both the Mórrígan and the banshee are similar to the Grim Reaper, who is well known in the United States as a being that appears at the time of death to gather souls.

However, the banshee is most often seen as a spirit wailing over an impending death during the night, which is not something the Mórrígan does. The banshee is also associated with mourning for a family she knows, while the Mórrígan isn't specific to a family lineage.

Many scholars think it's possible that the Mórrígan and the banshee overlap. The banshee may have been inspired by the Mórrígan at some point in ancient history. The charm of the Celtic myth is just this: there are many ways to draw connections between stories and characters, but plenty of ambiguity always remains to keep us guessing.

Would you like to know the actual folklore about the banshee, not just the mistaken rumors from pop culture?

A banshee is a female spirit who comes from the ancient burial mounds, known as the sidhe, where the fairies dwell. The banshee is considered a type of fairy, known as an omen of death who would follow certain ancient Irish families along their lineage for years and years. The banshee would appear before a family member died, weeping sadly. She wasn't malevolent, but she was thought to be a family friend who was genuinely sad that someone in the family was going to die.

The tradition of women keening or crying like a banshee became a part of Scottish and Irish funerals.

According to legend, the six ancient families of Ireland each had their own banshee, or female spirit, that acted as the harbinger of death for the family. The family names were the O'Neills, O'Donnells, O'Connors, O'Learys, O'Tools, and the O'Connaghs.

Some believe banshees are bird-like creatures. They were often seen perching on a windowsill like a bird, waiting for days until death arrived. As the banshee left the scene, fleeing into the darkness, many people described hearing a fluttering noise, adding to the idea that banshees had bird-like qualities.

She tended to appear as a young maiden, a stately matron, or a terrible old hag. This seems to correspond to the Mórrígan as a triple goddess, though the banshee wasn't a goddess. Typically the banshee would be wearing the clothing of a country woman, often white, but occasionally brown, red, gray, or green. The banshee's eyes were always red and swollen due to her constant weeping.

The banshee has long, blond hair that is almost white. She has been seen sitting and combing her hair as she wails. If you ever see a comb on the ground in Ireland, you should never pick it up. It could have been placed there by a banshee to lure unsuspecting humans. If you pick up the comb, a banshee could appear and spirit you far away, out of the human plane.

Some say this is a confusion with the Irish mermaid myths since both mermaids and banshees are associated with water, long hair, combs, and luring gullible humans.

Banshees can also be found wailing in nature. They appear at wooded locations, rocks, and rivers. In Ireland, there are famous wedge-shaped rocks known as "banshee's chairs." They're located in Waterford, Monaghan, and Carlow.

Have you ever seen a foxglove flower? Foxglove is extremely poisonous; even its pollen can cause a harmful reaction in some people. Otherwise nicknamed fairy thimble, foxglove is considered a flower of the sidhe and attributed to the banshee. In the Irish language, foxgloves are called *lus na mban sidhe*, which translates to "the plant of the banshee."

If a person lived a selfish, sinful life of decadence or committed cruel acts, it was believed the banshee would keep them close to the earth to suffer their punishment in the afterlife rather than allowing them to leave the mortal plane. If a person was good and kind in their lifetime, their soul could rest in peace and happiness for all of eternity. The banshee would assure this happened.

The sound the banshee makes is different depending on the location and who you ask. In Leinster, the banshee's sound is an ear-piercing scream that can break glass. In Kerry, her keening cry is described as a pleasant, low singing. In Tyrone, the banshee makes a loud sound like two boards being smacked together. On Rathlin Island, her sound is between the cry of an owl and wail of a woman.

Did you know you can capture a banshee and force her to give information? Folklore says she can be intimidated by the point of a sword or injured by cold-forged iron. She can also be repelled by salt.

The banshee has various Irish Gaelic names, including banshie, bean si, bean sidhe, and ban side. The two main words in Gaelic are *bean* and *sídhe*, which translates to "female fairy," or "woman of the Otherworld." In Munster and Connaught she is referred to as *bean chaointe*, which means "a female keener."

One of the oldest banshee stories is found in the *Memoirs of Lady Fanshawe* and Sir Walter Scott's *Lady of the Lake.*

The story takes place in the year 1642. Sir Richard and his wife, Lady Fanshawe, went to visit a friend who lived in a baron's castle. In the night, Lady Fanshawe was awakened by a piercing scream. When she opened her eyes, she saw a female face and half of a female figure illuminated in the moonlight, hovering at the window. Lady Fanshawe stared at the woman for what seemed like a long time. Finally, the apparition gave two shrieks and then vanished. The following morning, Lady Fanshawe told her terrifying story to their host. The host told her she had seen a banshee because that same night one of their family members had died in the castle.

Perhaps the most famous account of a person hearing a banshee wail was told by Ireland's last High King, Brian Boru. According to this legend, the banshee appeared in front of Boru's family. She wailed three times. (Remember, the number three is important to the Celtic people.) This foretold Boru's death in battle. The next day, Brian Boru was praying inside his tent when he was suddenly killed. His family knew right away they had experienced a banshee the night before, coming to warn of the High King's impending death.

Some say the first banshees came from the eighth century. Women were hired to be keeners (criers) at funerals. These women accepted alcohol as a form of payment, which made them sinful, and they were condemned to live forever as banshees.

The banshee is believed to be one of the Tuatha Dé Danann, as well. Brigid, the Tuatha Dé Danann goddess of fertility and poetry who heralds the spring and summer months each year beginning on Beltane, first began the tradition of keening and wailing at a death and at the funeral. Her keening wasn't just screaming and crying, however. It was poetic and structured, almost song-like.

The keening practice began with Brigid during the Second Battle of Moytura, also known as Cath Tánaiste Maige Tuired. The battle took place on the plains of Moytura between the Tuatha Dé Danann and the Fomorians. During the fighting, Brigid's son was tragically killed. When Brigid discovered his body on the battlefield, she wailed the most sorrowful cry from deep within her soul. It was a poetic, mournful cry that became a song to honor her son's death.

An Origin Story

One possible origin story for the banshee legend goes as follows.

On the northeastern shore of Lough Neagh, a castle sat for many centuries. Its original name was Eden-duff-carrick. In 1607, the castle was reinstated to the O'Neill clan who originally owned it, after which it was referred to as Shane's Castle.

In one of the tower walls, there is a stone carving of a head. This head is known as the "black head of the O'Neills," or the "black brow on the rock." The carving is thought to be older than the castle itself, and legend has it that the line of the O'Neills will come to an end if the head ever falls from the castle wall.

Luckily, the head survived intact on the wall when their banshee burned their castle!

It's said the O'Neills' banshee was created as an act of revenge on the part of the fairies. One of the ancient O'Neills was returning from a raid when he saw a cow with its horns tangled in the branches of a hawthorn tree. The hawthorn tree, when found growing alone, is sacred to the fairies. If a cow was tangled in one of their trees, then that cow now belonged to the fairies.

Unfortunately for the O'Neills, their ancestor decided to free the tangled cow. This enraged the fairies. The man continued on his walk home. At that time, the castle had not yet been built, but an older building stood in its place, presumably with the black brow on the rock. When the man arrived home, he found his daughter missing. To his dismay, he learned that the fairies had taken his daughter to the bottom of the lough.

The fairies allowed the little girl to return and tell her family she was safe in the fairy kingdom. However, after that, she was only allowed to return to alert the family to a death by keening and wailing.

It's believed her original name in the story was Maeve. Maeve's death and then her forced journey to the Otherworld fits perfectly with the folklore surrounding the fairies and the banshee.

This contributes to the legend that a banshee is a woman filled with peace who is tasked with watching over her loved ones and mourning their deaths, though they do have the anxiety-inducing ability to predict a death before it happens.

The castle continues to be steeped in lore. Richard Nash, the architect of Buckingham Palace, was renovating the castle when a fire broke out. The conservatory, which had already been renovated, survived the fire. Sadly, the main block of the castle was completely destroyed.

However, the head of the O'Neill family miraculously remained intact and hanging on the tower wall.

Today, the public can visit this famous castle and tour the grounds, including the O'Neill family tomb and statues. The banshee has been heard over the last few centuries in Coile Ultagh, the woods nearby the castle. Much of the area today has become farmland or housing developments, but a little of the original woods remains.

Today, we can spot the banshee in literature if we look carefully. For example, in *Wuthering Heights* by Emily Bronte, the character Cathy is said to be able to wail. Her mournful crying predicts that someone will die, which serves to enhance the mood of the novel, giving it a gloomy and foreboding feeling. *The Picture of Dorian Gray* by Oscar Wilde also features a banshee of sorts. Her name is Sibyl Vane. She makes a mournful banshee wail, which foretells the death of her love, Dorian Gray.

While no one knows the true origin of the banshee, one important fact remains: the banshee gives us fascinating clues into the way the Celts perceived death and the rituals surrounding it. It's a timeless myth that persists unchanged, even against modern pop culture's attempts to twist the banshee into a jump scare character.

Chapter 10: The Legacy of Irish Mythology

Irish mythology is far more than just a collection of fantasy stories from the ancient past. It has played an important role in the formation of Irish culture, shaped the geographic landscape of Ireland, and even touched the politics of the country. Irish lore is completely entangled in every aspect of what it means to be Irish.

The original Irish myths were part of the oral tradition passed down through storytelling and traveling bards. Ironically, the first people to put these beloved myths on paper were the Catholic monks who came to Ireland.

You might wonder why monks would write down the stories of the pagan gods that were so important to the Irish people. Writing down the myths and legends, while adding bits of Catholicism and monotheism into the stories, was one way the monks slowly incorporated Christianity into Irish culture. They used the gods and goddesses of Ireland to pave the way for the introduction of Christianity.

We see this in stories like the Children of Lir, when the children waited to hear a church bell ring at the end of the story, or in the later version of Oisín and Niamh's love story, when Oisín was taken to the famous St. Patrick after falling from his horse and becoming an old man.

St. Patrick is the patron saint of Ireland today. His role in Irish mythology has helped bridge the gap between polytheism and monotheism in Irish culture. In *Acallam na Senórach,* or Tales of the

Elders of Ireland, written at the end of the twelfth century, we find St. Patrick journeying through Ireland with Oisín and his nephew, Caílte mac Rónáin. Oisín and his nephew explain every cultural landmark, the significance of the names, and the history of each place to St. Patrick. The conversations between the three men meld together the ancient ways of pre-Christian Ireland with the new morals and religion of Christianity. Seamlessly, Irish mythology blended in and gave way to monotheism.

Some of the old gods and goddesses were relegated to being members of the sidhe, living under the mounds, but still very much revered and respected in whispers by the Irish people. Others, like Brigid, the Celtic goddess of spring, seem to have moved from goddess to Catholic saint. The monks needed to create stories that felt familiar to the Irish people, so Saint Brigid was born. No one knows if she was an actual person as there is no proof of her life other than the stories. The Christian feast on the day of her death and the celebration day of Imbolc for Brigid the goddess are one and the same, February 1. The goddess Brigid lives on today as the patroness saint of Ireland, an everlasting link to Ireland's ancient pre-Christian past.

Politically, Ireland has faced a long and arduous struggle for independence beginning in the sixteenth century when colonization by the English destroyed the country's autonomy. As the traditional Irish governing system of kings and kingdoms was torn down and forcefully replaced by a central British monarchy, Irish culture was changed forever.

One thing remained strong in the hearts and minds of the Irish people: their shared love for ancient history, their myths and folklore. Their hero Finn McCool and the undying reverence for the sidhe never left the Irish landscape. Irish heroes and myths were the glue holding together the Gaelic culture throughout hundreds of years of drastic changes and hardships.

After the Great Famine in 1845, Ireland faced one of its lowest points. Many Irish people had left the country, creating an Irish diaspora around the world. In some cases, entire families in Ireland had starved and died. The traditional Gaelic-speaking areas of the country were nearly completely lost.

During the struggle to survive, industrialization and English customs took over Ireland. Despite everything, bits of Irish lore remained intact, primarily the respect and fear of fairies. The landscape still contained geographic reminders of Ireland's pagan past. Places like the Giant's

Causeway or the fairy mounds scattered all over the country tied the people to their Gaelic culture, never letting them forget who they were or where their ancestors came from.

In the late nineteenth and early twentieth century, Ireland began to experience a revival of Gaelic culture. There was a renewed interest in Irish myths, art, music, and the Gaelic language. The movement, sweetly nicknamed Celtic Twilight, was closely aligned with the Irish Nationalist movement. In 1893, the Gaelic league was formed to focus on reviving the Irish language and culture.

Photo of W. B. Yeats.
https://commons.wikimedia.org/wiki/File:WB_Yeats_nd.jpg

The work of poet and playwright William Butler Yeats is possibly one of the most well-known examples of ancient Irish culture being revived and renewed for nineteenth and twentieth-century generations. His writings featured famous Irish heroes, including Oisín. His poems drew heavily from Irish myths and the Irish landscape, reintroducing readers to the mysterious world of the fairies and reminding everyone of Ireland's timeless beauty and unique history.

Yeats helped found the Abbey Theater, which was the first Irish national theater. While Yeats and other poets were sharing their writings based on Irish culture, something uniquely Irish happened. The stories of heroes, gods, goddesses, and the associated cultural pride inspired men to join forces and form an Irish nationalist group that desired to overthrow British rule.

This led to a secret brotherhood, called the Irish Republican Brotherhood (IRB), which planned one of the most significant events in all of Irish history: The 1916 Easter Rising.

The military council of the IRB procured weapons and made plans to fight back against the British. On April 24, 1916, the Proclamation of the Irish Republic was read out loud by Padraig Pearse in front of the General Post Office (GPO) in Dublin. In total, one thousand members of the IRB occupied the GPO and five other buildings around Dublin.

This sparked a battle between the Irish and the British that lasted several days. The British only had forces totaling four hundred men at the beginning of the fight. By April 28, the British had brought in 19,000 troops.

On April 29, 1916, the Irish rebels surrendered to prevent further bloodshed. The leaders of the Easter Rising were executed, including several Irish poets who played a role in inspiring the Irish nationalist movement.

This included Patrick Pearse, a bilingual writer, a teacher, and the first Provisional President of the Irish Republic. He founded the New Ireland Literary Society, which played a role in the nationalism that fueled the Easter Rising by spreading Irish folklore, poetry, and literature.

We can clearly see how closely Irish myths, language, and culture are tied to all of Ireland's history, even the tragic and infamous Easter Rising of 1916. Without Irish mythology, would Ireland have held together in the face of hundreds of years of British rule?

On a lighter note, Irish mythology has also shaped Western television and comics, showing up in places we may not even recognize. For example, Conan the Barbarian is based on Conán mac Morna, a member of the Fianna and frequent character in stories featuring Finn McCool.

Arnold Schwarzenegger played Conan the Barbarian in his 1982 and 1984 films, making Conan the Barbarian a household name in the United States.

Marvel Comics introduced Conan the Barbarian to readers in its first issue of *Savage Tales*. From there, Irish mythology continued to appear in Marvel comics, including in *The Mighty Thor* when the Tuatha Dé Danann made an appearance as a force to be reckoned with. In one part of the series, Thor even joins forces with Dagda to defeat a foe.

The *Hellboy* comic book series features Prince Nuada. Sound familiar? In Irish mythology, King Nuada loses his arm and has it replaced by a fully-functioning bionic limb.

The ever-popular *Game of Thrones* series heavily features ideas and character concepts from Irish mythology, though most readers are likely unaware of the ties. Bran Stark takes his name from the raven, which is often related to the name "Bran" in Celtic mythology. Bran Stark later transforms into the Celtic three-eyed raven.

Of course, we couldn't finish talking about present-day Irish culture without mentioning the timeless music of Ireland. The genre of Irish music has multiple branches, all which relate back to the history of ancient Ireland. Notably, there have been many modern songs, including rock songs, based on Irish myths like the Children of Lir or The Tale Of Cú Chulainn.

Irish mythology is the heartbeat of Ireland. It's the pulse that all of Ireland depends on, from the past to the present, continuing to beat strongly even through so many changes in modernization and lifestyle.

Conclusion

Throughout this book we've discussed the four cycles of Irish mythology: the Mythological Cycle, the Ulster Cycle, the Fenian cycle, and the King Cycle. Each one of these cycles contains timeless myths and legends that have forever shaped Ireland's arts, politics, culture, and people into who they are today. Through Irish mythology, we've met the formidable Mórrígan, the misunderstood banshee, the epic Irish hero Finn McCool, and many other side characters along the way.

More than just ancient stories, Irish myths and legends are alive. We can find these gods and goddesses influencing holidays, art, music, literature, and even heavily affecting Irish politics in recent years.

Through the chapters in this book, you can see how Irish folklore is a chain of links that continually connects people in the present to the past. Generations are held together with these links by a shared set of beliefs: faith in the great heroes and respect for the fairy realm.

How important is it for the Irish to continue preserving their cultural treasures? It is vital to their survival as a culture because their myths and legends give a window into their ancient past as well as a mirror to see the present.

Imagine an Ireland without the fairies and without the influence of our hero Finn and his warriors the Fianna. Would anything in Ireland be the same without Irish mythology?

Perhaps one of the most magical aspects of Irish folklore is its ability to continue growing, changing, and evolving rather than dying out over time. Despite the written mythology being readily available, new stories of banshee encounters or fairy magic are always being told, blending the old with the new and creating more diverse layers to add to the canon of Irish mythology. As scholar and author Diarmuid Ó Giolláin said, "New versions of old things are always appearing."[13]

---

[13] Ó Giolláin, Diarmuid. *Locating Irish Folklore: Tradition, Modernity, Identity.* Cork: Cork University Press, 2000.

If you enjoyed this book, a review on Amazon would be greatly appreciated because it would mean a lot to hear from you.

To leave a review:

1. Open your camera app.
2. Point your mobile device at the QR code.
3. The review page will appear in your web browser.

Thanks for your support!

Here's another book by Enthralling History that you might like

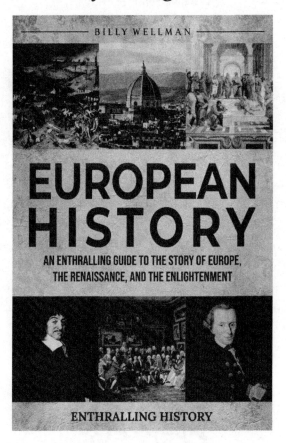

Free limited time bonus

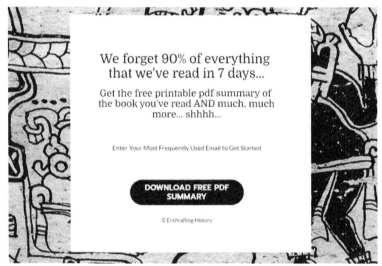

Stop for a moment. We have a free bonus set up for you. The problem is this: we forget 90% of everything that we read after 7 days. Crazy fact, right? Here's the solution: we've created a printable, 1-page pdf summary for this book that you're reading now. All you have to do to get your free pdf summary is to go to the following website: https://livetolearn.lpages.co/enthrallinghistory/

Or, Scan the QR code!

Once you do, it will be intuitive. Enjoy, and thank you!

Appendix A: Further Reading and Reference

Ashley, Mike. *The Giant Book of Myths and Legends.* 1995.

Cronin, Mike. *A History of Ireland.* 2001.

Foster, R. F. *The Oxford Illustrated History of Ireland.* 1989.

Gibney, John. *A Short History of Ireland: 1500-2000.* 2017.

Neville, Peter. *A Traveller's History of Ireland.* 1992.

O'Halloran, Marie. "Ireland Is Not Neutral About Ukraine." https://www.irishtimes.com/politics/2022/11/15/ireland-is-not-neutral-about-ukraine-taoiseach-insists-in-renewed-row-over-constitutional-position/.

Osborne-McKnight, Juilene. *The Story We Carry in Our Bones: Irish History for Americans.* 2015.

State, F. Paul. *A Brief History of Ireland.* 2009.

Atkins, Ruth. For Fear of Little Men- Podcast Script. https://unrealpodcast.com/for-fear-of-little-men-podcast-script/. 2024

Brehon Academy (2020). Aengus Og: The Irish God of Love. https://brehonacademy.org/aengus-og-the-irish-god-of-love/. 2024

Brehon Academy (2023). Heroic Biography: Finn McCool - A Giant of Irish Folklore and Tradition. https://brehonacademy.org/heroic-biography-finn-mccool-a-giant-of-irish-folklore-and-tradition/. 2024

Brehon Academy (2020). The Dream of Aengus (Aisling Oengus). https://brehonacademy.org/the-dream-of-angus-aisling-aengus/. 2024

Clark, Rosalind (1990). The Great Queens: Irish Goddesses from the Morrigan to Cathleen Ni Houlihan. Irish Literary Studies. 2024.

Connolly, Ciaran. Incredible History of the Tuatha de Danann: Ireland's Most Ancient Race (2024). https://www.connollycove.com/tuatha-de-danann/#the-theory-of-the-cave-fairies. 2024

Connolly, Ciaran (2024). The Fascinating Legends of Finn McCool and the Isle of Man. https://www.connollycove.com/legend-finn-mccool-isle-man/. 2024

ConnollyCove (2023). Beware the Wail of the Banshee - This Irish Fairy Isn't as Scary as You Think. https://www.connollycove.com/banshee/. 2024

ConnollyCove (2024). The Children of Lir: A Fascinating Irish Legend. https://www.connollycove.com/children-of-lir/. 2024

Croker, Thomas Crofton (1828). The Merrow Fairy Legends and Traditions of the South of Ireland. Vol. Part II. 2024

Cuerbo, Maria J Perez (2018). The Bizarre Death of Bridget Cleary, The Irish Fairy Wife

Gulermovich Epstein, Angelique (1998). War Goddess: The Morrigan and Her Germano-Celtic Counterparts. 2024

Ireland Information (1998-2007). Aine the Goddess Who Took Revenge on a King. https://www.ireland-information.com/irish-mythology/aine-irish-legend.html. 2024

Irish Padan School Admin. The Sidhe - Irish Fairy Folklore (2022). https://irishpagan.school/sidhe-irish-fairy-folklore/. 2024

Kinsella, Thomas. 1969. How the Tain Bo Cuailnge Was Found Again, The Tain. 2024

McGrath, Stuart (2023). 1916 Rising: 1916 Rising: Facts, figures & Infographic. https://www.claddaghrings.com/1916-infographic/. 2024

Monstropedia (2011). Banshee. https://www.monstropedia.org/index.php?title=Banshee. 2024

O'Connell, H. & Doyle, P.G. (2006). The Burning of Cleary: Psychiatric Aspects of a Tragic Tale. Irish Journal of Medical Science. 2024

Ó Giolláin, Diarmuid (2000). Locating Irish Folklore: Tradition, Modernity, Identity. Cork: Cork University Press. 2024

Ross, Anne (1967). Pagan Celtic Britain: Studies in Iconography. 2024

Schirmer, Melissa (2014). The Irish Literary Revival. https://libapps.libraries.uc.edu/exhibits/irish-lit/sample-page/. 2024

ShanOre Irish Jewelry. Triskele: Unveiling this Enigmatic Celtic Symbol: An Ancient Celtic Symbol of Life, Death, and Rebirth (2023). https://www.shanore.com/blog/triskele-meaning/#:~:text=The%20number%20three%20held%20special,heaven%2C%20earth%2C%20and%20purgatory. 2024

Wright, Gregory. Cailleach (2022). https://mythopedia.com/topics/cailleach. 2024

Printed in Great Britain
by Amazon

43535677R00106